This strategy-rich text on interactive reading adopts a broadened definition of literacy that is inclusive of all learners with extensive support needs. Guidance is provided on how to conduct comprehensive assessments that acknowledge the impact of motor abilities, functional hearing, functional vision, and tactile skills on communication and literacy development. The text guides readers to develop and deliver interactive reading lessons that address all aspects of literacy from book handling to vocabulary and comprehension. New and experienced professionals will find this text to be an indispensable teaching tool.
–Susan M. Bruce, Ph.D., Boston College

Brum provides teachers with practical, evidence-based strategies to support learners with extensive support needs in attaining meaningful literacy goals. Educators who want to extend their impact and help their students achieve greater reading outcomes will value the useful advice on increasing comprehension, communication, and overall literacy to advance inclusion and independence.
–Christopher J. Lemons, Ph.D., Stanford University

Interactive Reading for Learners with Extensive Support Needs

This comprehensive guidebook shows teachers how to implement high-quality evidence-based interactive reading lessons for children with extensive support needs. It features step-by-step instructions for developing, implementing, and assessing shared reading lessons that are meaningful, engaging, and supportive of this population's needs across cognitive, sensory, physical, and behavioral domains. Featuring templates to help readers organize critical information needed to plan and implement each lesson, as well as sample assessments to help identify learner interests, identify baseline skills, and monitor progress, the book is both practical and widely applicable across grade bands and curricula. *Interactive Reading for Learners with Extensive Support Needs* is key reading for teachers and literacy coaches who work with children with complex support needs, as well as faculty in personnel preparation programs in the areas of sensory disabilities, severe disabilities, and special education.

Christopher Brum, Ph.D., is Associate Professor of Special Education at San Diego State University. He started his career as a special education teacher and currently leads professional development sessions for teachers focused on the implementation of high-quality and evidence-based teaching practices for learners with disabilities.

Other Eye on Education Books Available from Routledge
(www.routledge.com/eyeoneducation)

Reimagining the Role of Teachers in Nature-based Learning
Helping Children be Curious, Confident, and Caring
Rachel Larimore and Claire Warden

Promoting Language and Early Literacy Development
Practical Insights from a Parent Researcher
Pamela Beach

Teaching Higher-Order Thinking to Young Learners, K–3
How to Develop Sharp Minds for the Disinformation Age
Steffen Saifer

Everyday STEAM for the Early Childhood Classroom
Integrating the Arts into STEM Teaching
Margaret Loring Merrill

A New Vision for Early Childhood
Rethinking Our Relationships with Young Children
Noah Hichenberg

Interactive Reading for Learners with Extensive Support Needs
A Practical Guide for Teachers

Christopher Brum

Routledge
Taylor & Francis Group
NEW YORK AND LONDON

Designed cover image: shutterstock

First published 2025
by Routledge
605 Third Avenue, New York, NY 10158

and by Routledge
4 Park Square, Milton Park, Abingdon, Oxon, OX14 4RN

Routledge is an imprint of the Taylor & Francis Group, an informa business

© 2025 Taylor & Francis

The right of Christopher Brum to be identified as author of this work has been asserted in accordance with sections 77 and 78 of the Copyright, Designs and Patents Act 1988.

All rights reserved. No part of this book may be reprinted or reproduced or utilised in any form or by any electronic, mechanical, or other means, now known or hereafter invented, including photocopying and recording, or in any information storage or retrieval system, without permission in writing from the publishers.

Trademark notice: Product or corporate names may be trademarks or registered trademarks, and are used only for identification and explanation without intent to infringe.

ISBN: 9781032858357 (hbk)
ISBN: 9781032858364 (pbk)
ISBN: 9781003520030 (ebk)

DOI: 10.4324/9781003520030

Typeset in Palatino
by Deanta Global Publishing Services, Chennai, India

Contents

Meet the Author x
Preface xi
Acknowledgments xiii
List of Abbreviations xiv

1 Literacy for Learners with Extensive Support Needs 1

   Characteristics of Individuals with Extensive
   Support Needs 1
      Identifying Learner Assets and Areas of Support 2
   Literacy for Students with Extensive Support Needs 4
   Literacy and Language Goal Development 6
   Supporting the Learner's Identity During Instruction 8
   Students with Sensory Impairments 10
      Deaf/Hard of Hearing 10
      Visual Impairment 11
      Deafblindness 12
   Conclusion 13
   References 13

**2 Communication Development for Learners with
   Extensive Support Needs** 18

   Communication Development 18
   Strategies for Supporting Communication
   Development During Literacy Instruction 21
      Reflexive Partners 21
      Consistency 22
      Integrating Opportunities 23
      Environmental Regulation 25
      Pairing Communication Forms 27
   Students with Sensory Impairments 28
   Augmentative and Alternative Communication 29
      Tangible Symbols 30
      Strategies for Implementing AAC 32

Conclusion 34
References 35

**3 Assessment for Learners with Extensive
Support Needs** 37

Assessment Considerations for Individuals
with Extensive Support Needs 37
  Personal Characteristics 39
Students with Sensory Impairment 40
  Functional Vision and Learning Media Assessment 40
  Tactile Skills Assessment 42
  Informal Functional Hearing Evaluation 42
Communication Assessment 43
  Communication Complexity Scale 43
  Communication Matrix 47
Foundational Literacy Skill Assessment 50
Literacy-Rich Environments 53
Student Interest 54
Professional Collaboration 54
Assessment Resources 56
Conclusion 57
References 57

4 Lesson Planning and Material Preparation 61

Comprehensive Lesson Planning 61
  Part A: Learner Assets and Areas of Support 62
  Part B: Literacy Skills and Instructional Goals 65
  Part C: Lesson Preparation 66
Conclusion 79
References 80

5 Implementing Interactive Reading 82

Systematic Instruction 83
  Securing the Learner's Attention 83
  Prompts 84
  Instructional Trials 88
Vocabulary Development 88
  Selecting Vocabulary for Instruction 88
  Introducing Vocabulary 90

    Building Scaffolding Through Constant Time Delay 91
    Developing Emergent Literacy Skills 92
    Supporting Reading Comprehension 93
        Gaining the Learner's Attention 93
        Activating Prior Knowledge 93
        Reading Intentions 94
        Integrating Comprehension Questions 95
    Connection to Lesson Plan. 97
    Conclusion 99
    References. 100

**6 Comprehensive Progress Monitoring to Inform
   Instruction** 103

    Instructional Goals and Objectives. 103
        Phases of Learning. 104
        Selecting Behaviors or Skills to Teach 106
    Writing High-Quality Learning Goals. 108
    Using Data to Inform Instruction 109
        Data Collection 110
        Data-Based Decision Making 114
        Instructional Changes and Building Complexity 115
    Conclusion 117
    References. 118

**7 Developing and Sustaining Opportunities for
   Inclusion**. 120

    Successful Inclusion 121
        Universal Design for Learning 121
        Collaborative Teaming. 122
        Peer-Mediated Supports 122
    Planning for Inclusion. 125
        Aided AAC Modeling 125
        Supporting Inclusion During Literacy Instruction 127
    Conclusion 127
    References. 129

    Appendix A: Comprehensive Lesson Planning Template. 131
    Appendix B: Interactive Reading Data Collection Sheet 136

Meet the Author

Christopher Brum, Ph.D., is Associate Professor with the Department of Special Education at San Diego State University and directs the Liberal Studies undergraduate program at SDSU. Dr. Brum began his career as an inner-city special education teacher. He received both his master's degree in Severe Disabilities/Deafblindness and later a doctorate in Curriculum and Instruction from Boston College. He completed a graduate fellowship with the Hellen Keller Fellows and a doctoral fellowship with the National Leadership Consortium on Sensory Disabilities (NLCSD) with a concentration in deafblindness. Dr. Brum's areas of interest include communication and literacy development for complex learners, specifically related to deafblindness, autism, and low-incidence disabilities, and supporting teachers and paraprofessionals to implement high-quality and evidence-based practices.

Preface

My career in education began as an inner-city special education teacher working with elementary students with extensive support needs. In my classroom, reading became the way we connected with one another. I still remember watching the anticipation build in my students as their favorite part of the story approached, sometimes so much that they physically could not stay in their seats. The excitement, the engagement, the interactions, most often without formal language, but always with animation and fun. We used whatever we could find to bring a book to life, mostly including thrift store finds, hand-me-downs, and dollar store treasures. The excitement for reading spread beyond me and the students, and soon, the paraprofessionals, related service personnel, and even administrators were added to the mix, either joining us in the reading circle or contributing items for one of our favorite stories. One of my fondest memories is one of our occupational therapists bursting into the classroom with a smile ear to ear and carrying a large bag overflowing with about 20 different hats and monkey costumes to accompany a story about a peddler selling his wares.

Reading not only brought us all together as a classroom community, but it also served as a vehicle for change. Over those years, we all worked together to support our students in making great gains in their academic, communication, and functional skills. We would sit at lunch as a team and discuss ideas for the next book. Everyone contributed ideas: the speech-language pathologist with vocabulary to integrate, the occupational therapist about a sensory extension activity, the physical therapist with positioning suggestions, and the paraprofessionals with suggestions about stories related to student interests. Together, we all worked as a team to make books come alive for the students, and we watched as they grew and developed.

Understanding the power of reading led me back to school to start researching how literacy can support outcomes for students with extensive support needs, including individuals with visual impairment, hearing loss, and deafblindness. Although I am no longer an elementary school special educator, today, I have the privilege of training our pre-service special education teachers and doing my best to get them excited about the power of reading.

This is not a textbook. Seriously. It's a guide to making reading work for your learners with extensive support needs. The book is filled with tips, tricks, and lessons learned from my years as a special education teacher and now as a university professor. I hope the information inside helps you to build amazing connections with your students so that you can support them to make some great gains. Remember, it's just a book filled with suggestions, so take and use what works for you and your students. Happy reading!

Acknowledgments

This book would not have been possible without all of the students, teachers, and colleagues who have influenced and taught me throughout the years. A special thanks to Susan, my teacher, mentor, and friend who has always supported me by sharing her encouragement, knowledge, and, most importantly, her time. Throughout this process, she helped me think through ideas, read through chapter drafts, and encouraged me to keep going. Thank you to Diana for letting me use her excellent book about Ed Roberts. Also, I could not have finished this book without my friends and colleagues, especially Laura and Sam, who shared their home with me to hide away and furiously write. Lastly, and, most importantly, I owe thanks to my family, who gave me the time and space I needed to dedicate to this project.

List of Abbreviations

AAC	Augmentative and alternative communication
AT	Assistive technology
COMS	Certified orientation and mobility specialist
FVA	Functional vision assessment
IEP	Individualized education program
Learner	Individual with extensive support needs
LMA	Learning media assessment
OT	Occupational therapist
PT	Physical therapist
SGD	Speech-generating device
SLP	Speech-language pathologist
TOD	Teacher of the deaf and hearing impaired
TVI	Teacher of the blind and visually impaired
UDL	Universal design for learning

1

Literacy for Learners with Extensive Support Needs

There is no single (or easy) way to describe a learner with extensive support needs. The individuals within this population are unique, and, because of this, the supports and services they receive and the locations where these are provided can vary immensely even from classroom to classroom. This can make it very challenging for teachers to identify how to support these students and do it in a way that will allow them meaningful interaction and engagement during an important activity, such as a literacy lesson. Before exploring how to engage and support individuals with extensive support needs in an interactive literacy lesson, we need to look at how the population is defined and some key characteristics.

Characteristics of Individuals with Extensive Support Needs

Learners with extensive support needs describes a heterogeneous group of individuals that has diverse abilities, experiences, and areas where they require support (Westling et al., 2021). This can describe individuals with moderate to severe intellectual disability, which may be paired with an additional disability, such as autism or cerebral palsy, that require ongoing support for more than one major life activity (Bruce et al., 2024). The overall

DOI: 10.4324/9781003520030-1

development is often further impacted by health issues, physical disabilities, communication struggles, and behavioral challenges, as well as sensory impairments, such as vision and/or hearing losses. This results in a complex and multiplicative set of implications that are far greater than simply adding up the implications of each disability while also increasing vulnerability and exclusion based on perceived limitations rather than identifying and capitalizing on the individual's strengths (Giangreco et al., 2020). That being said, it is important to closely examine some of the common areas of needed support, such as communication development and sensory considerations. A shared characteristic for individuals with extensive support needs is the need for ongoing support for more than one major life area, such as communication and language, movement and mobility, and activities of daily living, such as self-care, eating, and dressing. Pervasive health concerns are also common and can affect daily functioning, attention, and engagement during school (Heller, 2017).

Sensory impairments are common among individuals with extensive support needs, with an estimated 60% having a visual impairment and approximately 40% of individuals who are deaf or hard of hearing reporting at least one additional disability (Bruce et al., 2024). Similarly, when considering individuals with concurrent vision and hearing losses, or deafblindness, 87% indicate they possess at least one additional disability. These estimates highlight the importance for teachers, related service personnel, and families to attend to how the individuals with extensive support needs they serve utilize their vision and hearing abilities to ensure necessary supports can be implemented to support optimal access to instruction, materials, and the learning environment.

Identifying Learner Assets and Areas of Support
The concept of asset-based pedagogies, or strengths-based instruction, considers the diversity (culture, disability, home life, and personal characteristics) students bring into the classroom and marks a shift from the deficit-based model of instruction that focused on what students were not able to do (Llopart & Esteban-Guitart, 2018). This instructional starting point considers what a

student brings into the learning environment as an asset, including their diversity in cognition, intelligence, culture, traits, and experiences, encompassing related concepts such as Funds of Knowledge, Culturally Relevant and Sustaining Pedagogies, as well as Culturally and Linguistically Responsive Teaching (California Department of Education, 2024). For students with disabilities, asset-based learning has positively impacted academic, behavioral, and social-emotional outcomes, as well as improvements in self-advocacy, communication, and overall happiness (White et al., 2023). In addition to a focus on student strengths and what they can successfully accomplish, asset-based learning also focuses on student interests and preferences. Overall, all students bring diverse assets and areas where they require more attention and support into the classroom. This can include their prior experience with the content, preferences, and interests, as well as the implications of their disability.

Assessment from an asset-based perspective can include a balance of strengths and weaknesses to help obtain an understanding of the complexity of how the individual functions (Niemiec & Tomasulo, 2023). When considering a functional approach to asset-based assessment for learners with disabilities, consider the approach outlined by Buntinx (2013):

- **Functioning:** Assess strengths and weaknesses in functioning, including areas of strength, necessary supports, sensory impairment(s), and health concerns
- **Interest and Preference:** Assess ambitions, desires, and personal preferences, as well as likes and dislikes related to activities, media (movies, shows, reading material), and hobbies
- **Personal Goals:** Identify short- and long-term goals the individual possesses and the activities, supports, and resources necessary to accomplish each goal
- **Current Supports:** Across all areas of functioning, especially communication, mobility, and visual/auditory access, what supports does the individual have in place, and are the supports successful in improving the individual's quality of life?

Literacy for Students with Extensive Support Needs

When literacy is described broadly as one's ability to read and write, learners with extensive support needs can be immediately excluded from participating in this critical life activity. On the other hand, emergent literacy is often considered the prerequisite phase to conventional literacy, including concepts of print, meaning of text, and phonological awareness, with many students with extensive support needs being engaged in literacy instruction that focuses solely on sight word instruction or a teacher reading to students (Ahlgrim-Delzell & Rivera, 2015). More recently, these definitions have been expanded to be more inclusive of learners with complex needs, including those with intellectual disabilities, as well as learners with sensory impairments, such as visual impairment, deafness, or deafblindness (Luckner et al., 2016). For individuals with extensive support needs, the traditional definition of literacy is expanded to include reading, writing, listening, and speaking – heightening the focus on communication skills and embedding literacy within the immediate environment (Ruppar, 2015). This expanded definition extends literacy beyond print to include broader interactions with text using multiple forms of communication and technology.

Limited literacy skills can create educational, social, and communicative barriers that can have long-term impacts on overall development and quality of life. Given the intense focus on literacy in the early school years, this is especially important for young children. Literacy-based communication interventions have the potential to serve as engaging and effective means of improving language abilities for a broad range of learners (Murphy et al., 2022). Improved reading and writing skills lead to better communication skills for all individuals, including those with extensive support needs (Ricketts et al., 2013).

For learners with extensive support needs, including deafblindness, literacy instruction is grounded upon and begins with a comprehensive assessment of not only literacy skills but also sensory abilities (functional levels of vision and hearing), communication abilities, assistive technology supports, and learning media (Bruce & Brum, 2025). Outcomes of literacy instruction for learners with extensive support needs should primarily focus on improving life outcomes through shared interactions with literature and increasing independence as a reader (Ahlgrim-Delzell, 2020). Improving quality-of-life outcomes includes the interaction occurring between a student with extensive support needs and their partner when a text is being read together and information gained from the content of what was read. This includes physical and cognitive access to material, specifically related to the type of media (print, braille, audio), the level of complexity that can be easily understood by the learner, and the ways in which the individual will access the content (e.g., through a physical book, digitally, or through audio).

Specific guidelines for literacy instruction for learners with extensive support needs focus on planning and implementing literacy instruction to help reinforce the strong relationship between literacy and communication development for this population (Copeland et al., 2018). These guidelines include:

- **Maintain high expectations at all times.** Teacher beliefs impact instruction and student outcomes.
- **Deliver individualized, systematic, and consistent instruction.** Even when progress is slow, well-planned and intentional instruction is the most effective to teach new skills.
- **Integrate language and communication supports.** This includes integrating meaningful opportunities for communication throughout the entire activity, not just at the end to respond to questions.
- **Begin literacy learning in the early years.** The benefits of engaging in literacy start as early as infancy, so it is never too early (or too late) to start.
- **Literacy instruction should be comprehensive.** This means intentional efforts to teach emergent literacy skills as well as all the core components of literacy: phonemic awareness, phonics, fluency, vocabulary, and comprehension.
- **Learning to read is similar for everyone.** Individuals with extensive support needs follow a similar trajectory for literacy learning with their grade level peers and should have many opportunities to learn together rather than in isolation.

Interactive book reading, also known as shared reading, is a widespread practice where adults read a text to a child while posing questions, commenting, or expanding on information from the book to support a communicative interaction with the child about the content of the text (Fisher et al., 2004). For learners with extensive support needs, interactive reading supports engagement in age-appropriate text and serves as an effective vehicle to systematically teach vocabulary emergent literacy skills and develop comprehension (Toews et al., 2021). For individuals with extensive support needs, interactive book reading also has a strong connection with communication development. Throughout an interactive book-reading activity, the learner and facilitator have multiple and frequent opportunities to communicate about specific aspects of the content but can also share comments, ask questions, and seek more information. One easy way to ensure meaningful and sustained communicative interactions throughout the interactive reading activity is by targeting learner interest.

> Chapter 3 contains detailed assessment protocols and guidelines on how to assess different types of strengths to support literacy instruction for learners with extensive support needs.
> This includes assessing learner communication, interests and preferences, and literacy skills.

Literacy and Language Goal Development

Given the strong connection between literacy and communication, the crosscutting themes of Literacy and English Language Development Instruction (Slowik et al., 2015) can be helpful when developing instructional goals that support literacy and communication development for learners with extensive support needs. These include:

- *Meaning Making:* Whether interacting with or producing text, discussing a topic, or presenting information, meaning making focuses on gaining information from the materials, interactions, and communication involved in reading and writing, as well as the ability to recognize letters and words so that they can eventually be used to express words and ideas.

- *Language Development:* Language and communication, including reading, writing, speaking, and listening, are inherent to literacy and learning. Together, they contribute to learning and thinking, as well as the ability to seek and express information, pose questions, and understand the perspectives of others.
- *Effective Expression:* Self-expression through writing, discussion, presenting, and displaying information, as well as experiencing how others use language, supports the learner's expressive communication through writing and speaking across different environments and activities.
- *Content Knowledge:* Understanding the content is critical for comprehension and understanding the conventions of language to express one's ideas. It includes how individuals learn and organize information and is interwoven with literacy and language.
- *Foundational Skills:* For learners to effectively understand how to read and utilize written language, they must understand foundational skills, which include print concepts, phonological awareness, phonics and word recognition, and fluency.

When applying the crosscutting themes to learners with extensive support needs, they can be expanded to include augmentative and alternative communication (AAC) that supports self-expression and allows learners to more effectively demonstrate their understanding of literacy (Collins et al., 2024). Creating learning goals across these themes can ensure an instructional focus that simultaneously supports the development of communication and literacy abilities.

Comprehension is an essential aspect of language and literacy for all individuals, including learners with extensive support needs, and can be separated into listening comprehension and reading comprehension (Hudson, 2020). *Listening comprehension* includes one's ability to understand and make meaning of language, for example, understanding a story that is being read to you, while reading comprehension derives meaning from text through the process of decoding. The National Reading Panel (NRP, 2000) identified strategies for teaching comprehension to students without disabilities. These strategies are also relevant to learners with extensive support needs and include comprehension monitoring, cooperative learning, graphic and semantic organizers, generating and answering questions, and summarizing information. When planning literacy instruction for learners with extensive support needs, it is important to determine which comprehension skills the learner will focus on developing.

Supporting the Learner's Identity During Instruction

Leveraging students' background knowledge and connecting learning with students' experiences and interests is essential when working with a diverse group of learners (California Department of Education, 2024). This includes drawing on students' primary language and home culture when selecting materials and preparing lesson plans. In doing so, educators affirm and sustain the cultural backgrounds of students. Many of these students are also English learners tasked with learning a new language and academic content simultaneously. Thus, it is imperative that educators developing interventions for this population of learners are equipped to serve these culturally and linguistically diverse students by implementing culturally sustaining pedagogy. Culturally affirming pedagogy goes beyond culturally responsive pedagogy by both making connections to students' cultural knowledge and experiences and viewing schools and classrooms as places where culture is sustained (McCarty & Lee, 2014). Not incorporating culture into the development or adaptation of an intervention may lead to low sustainability or relevance to specific groups.

Individuals with extensive support needs are entitled to express their personal identity, which can positively impact self-determination and quality of life; however, communication challenges can often limit opportunities for identity expression (Wofford et al., 2022). As you will learn in the next chapter, individuals with extensive support often rely on alternative modes of communication, including nonverbal forms of communication, such as conventional and/or unconventional gestures, vocalizations, communication boards, and/or voice-generating devices (Beukelman & Light, 2020). Thus, communication interventions for individuals with extensive support needs, including supports such as AAC, should be grounded in an identity-focused framework that incorporates personal, social, and cultural identities (Ogletree et al., 2022; Wofford et al., 2022). Personal identity evolves over time and is unique to the person and their lived experiences. It encompasses unique self-expression through storytelling through verbal (or AAC) expression that can vary in tone and include social constructs like humor, affection, and intimacy. Social identity includes the interaction the individual has with their communication partners while also equipping them with the language to support different types of relationships, such as with family, friends, colleagues, and community members. The final aspect of the framework is cultural identity, which includes the individual's linguistic, racial, and ethnic background and also extends to include their gender identity, sexuality, and identity as a disabled person who uses AAC.

Literacy can serve as a means of supporting intersecting identities for individuals with extensive support needs, and students who speak another language may benefit from support in their native language (Lim et al., 2019). Core principles for providing heritage language support for culturally and linguistically individuals with extensive support needs (de Valenzuela, 2018).
  Strategies include:

- **Provide instruction in a language the student understands.** Instruction in any content area is only effective when the student can comprehend the input being provided. When there is a mismatch, students are left to make their own assumptions about meaning across languages, which can add additional and unnecessary cognitive load for students with extensive support needs.
- **Learning can transfer across languages.** Often, with just vocabulary support, students can easily transfer what they have learned from one language to another. This requires support staff who are proficient in the student's first language to be able to preview the content or support the language connections throughout the lesson.
- **Intentionally use different languages during instruction.** Plan ahead on when to use a student's home language to preview content and vocabulary, deciding which concepts can easily transfer across languages, and which should be taught in English or the student's home language.

Students with Sensory Impairments

The interconnectedness of language and literacy can create additional challenges for individuals with sensory impairments (Allen & Morere, 2020). This is especially true for learners who are deaf/hard of hearing, as well as those who are deafblind, as limited access to communication models impacts overall communication development, especially in the early years of life. This section will identify factors impacting literacy instruction for learners who are deaf/hard of hearing, visually impaired, or deafblind and provide a summary to support each population of learners during literacy instruction.

Deaf/Hard of Hearing

Many children, approximately 95%, who are deaf/hard of hearing are born to hearing parents, creating an immediate barrier to the critical language models that occur during infancy (Mitchell & Karchmer, 2004). However, when parents learn American Sign Language (ASL) alongside their children, age-expected vocabulary can reliably develop to create a foundation for future language and literacy development (Caselli et al., 2021). Because of the important role hearing serves in literacy development, especially when using phonological understanding (i.e., letter sounds) to decode words, literacy instruction for children who are deaf/hard of hearing differs for students who have functional hearing from children with limited functional hearing (Beal et al., 2024). For students with functional hearing, literacy instruction follows the traditional literacy instruction (NRP, 2000) on phonemic awareness, phonics, fluency, vocabulary, and comprehension, while, for students without functional hearing, the program is supplemented with fingerspelling and hand cues that represent phonemes.

Summary of strategies to support individuals who are deaf/hard of hearing during literacy instruction:

- ♦ Explicit instruction on strategies for comprehension, sight word identification, and morphemic analysis

- Continuous development of vocabulary across forms (speech, print, pictures, ASL) through dialog and conversation before, during, and after reading
- Activating students' prior knowledge and interests when selecting materials that are not overly simplified and include relevant vocabulary
- Teaching elements of a story, such as narrative structure or story grammar, and directed reading-thinking activities.

Visual Impairment

For students with visual impairment, literacy instruction aligns with the NRP's (2000) five principles but also maintains a focus on providing optimal access to print through traditional or alternative means, for example, using braille or large print to access the content (Luckner et al., 2016). For individuals using braille, early exposure is critical, and braille fluency has been positively connected to adult employment (Ferrell et al., 2014). Effective braille instruction follows a systematic drill and practice format and includes the introduction of contractions (Herzberg et al., 2017). Students with visual impairment also benefit from direct instruction to access print, braille, tactile graphics, or comprehension during auditory reading (Zebehazy & Wilton, 2014). For print readers, book handling (left-to-right orientation, top-to-bottom, and page-turning), comprehension, reading speed (silent and oral), and reading length have been linked to training and skills for using low-vision devices (REF). Students with visual impairment who read print require ongoing assessment and intervention to correctly use low-vision devices to optimize their functional vision capabilities (Luckner et al., 2016).

Summary of strategies to support individuals with visual impairments during literacy instruction:

- Repeated readings and exposure to a variety of genres
- Direct instruction on phonics and decoding morphemes
- Continuous focus on vocabulary development that extends beyond the early grades
- Early exposure to braille with a focus on prerequisite skill development, such as book handling skills

- Systematic instruction on braille code that includes drill and practice to improve fluency and comprehension
- Incorporating low-vision devices to improve access to print and advance reading speed and comprehension abilities

Deafblindness

Literacy instruction for individuals who are deafblind extends to include communication development, and many learners do not move past the prelinguistic phase of language development (Bruce & Brum, 2025). Literacy lessons for prelinguistic learners offer opportunities to simultaneously develop their communication and literacy skills and include daily schedules to develop anticipation, personalized story boxes developed with individualized representations to enhance understanding, opportunities to experience books that are co-developed with the learner to support the concept of distancing, and authentic and frequent opportunities for choice-making (Bruce et al., 2016). Literacy skill development can even be integrated into the daily schedule or activity sequence boards, teaching left-to-right and top-to-bottom orientation. Literacy-rich environments are critical for this group of learners, and students specifically benefit from access and frequent contact with books that include multiple representations (print, braille, tactile symbols, and objects), concurrent input that crosses multiple sensory channels (vision, hearing, touch), and consistent access to AAC and familiar communication partners (Brum & Bruce, 2023a).

Brum and Bruce (2023b) outlined specific strategies to support individuals who are deafblind during literacy instruction:

- Utilize interest to secure the individual's attention and maintain engagement and interaction throughout the activity.
- Employ child-guided strategies that include personalized literacy experiences, coactive movement, and emotional attunement.
- Integrate supports for vocabulary acquisition, including representations paired with specific communication forms that involve access through multiple sensory channels (e.g., object paired with a verbal label).

- Provide systematic instruction that includes wait time, the integration of prompting hierarchies, reinforcement, appropriate pacing, specific feedback, and is delivered in a highly structured and routine format.

Conclusion

Here are some points to consider when thinking about literacy for learners with extensive support needs:

- Plan literacy instruction that integrates meaningful opportunities for the learner to communicate throughout the planned activities. Consult the SLP from the beginning to support the integration of communication skill development into literacy learning.
- Be creative with literacy instruction and move beyond foundational skills and comprehension. Think about how the learner can capitalize on their strengths to make connections with what is read and express their understanding of the material.
- Build connections with the learner's family to authentically connect to their culture and identity. Simple efforts, such as connecting to family events or reading a favorite book from home can create meaningful connections.
- When beginning to plan instruction, always consider how the learner will access the information using multiple sensory channels. Collaborate with related service personnel to support the learner in maximizing their visual, auditory, and tactile sensory channels.

References

Ahlgrim-Delzell, L. (2020). Building early literacy and reading skills. In D. M. Browder, F. Spooner, & G. R. Courtade (Eds.), *Teaching students with moderate and severe disabilities* (2nd ed., pp. 143–159). Guilford Press.

Ahlgrim-Delzell, L., & Rivera, C. (2015). A content comparison of literacy lessons from 2004 and 2010 for students with moderate and severe intellectual disabilities. *Exceptionality, 23*, 258–269.

Allen, T. E., & Morere, D. A. (2020). Early visual language skills affect the trajectory of literacy gains over a three-year period of time for preschool aged deaf children experience signing in the home. *PLoS ONE, 15*(2), e0229591.

Beal., J. S., Dostal., H. M., & Easterbrooks, S. R. (2024). *Literacy instruction for students who are deaf and hard of hearing* (2nd ed.). Oxford Academic.

Beukelman, D. R., & Light, J.C. (2020). *Augmentative & alternative communication supporting children and adults with complex communication needs* (5th ed.). Paul H. Brookes Publishing Co.

Bruce, S., & Brum, C. (2025). Emergent literacy in individuals who are deafblind. In T. Hartshorne, M. J. Janssen, & W. Wittich (Eds.), *Volume II: Learning, education and support of deafblind children and adults: An interdisciplinary approach. Series: Perspectives in deafness.* Oxford University Press.

Bruce, S. M. & Ivy, S. E., & Brum, C. (2024). Severe and multiple disabilities. In J.M. Kauffman, D.P. Hallahan, & P.C. Pullen (Eds.), *Handbook of special education* (3rd ed.). Routledge.

Bruce, S. M., Nelson, C., Perez, A., Stutzman, B., & Barnhill, B. A. (2016). The state of research on communication and literacy in deafblindness. *American Annals of the Deaf, 161*(4), 424–443.

Brum, C., & Bruce, S. M. (2023a). Shared reading with learners who are deafblind: Instructional materials and learning environments. *Journal of Visual Impairment & Blindness, 117*(6), 418–428.

Brum, C., & Bruce, S. M. (2023b). Instructional strategies to support shared reading with learners who are deafblind. *British Journal of Visual Impairment, 41*(3), 504–516.

Buntinx, W. H. E. (2013). Understanding disability: A strengths-based approach. In M.L. Wehmeyer (Ed.), *The Oxford handbook of positive psychology and disability* (pp. 7–18). Oxford University Press.

California Department of Education (CDE). (2024). Asset-Based Pedagogies - Professional Learning. Retrieved from https://www.cde.ca.gov/ci/pl/assetbasedpedagogies.asp

Caselli, N., Pyers, J., & Lieberman, A. M. (2021). Deaf children of hearing parents have age-level vocabulary growth when exposed to

American Sign Language by 6 months of age. *The Journal of Pediatrics, 232,* 229–236.

Collins, S. C., Barton-Hulsey, A., Timm-Fulkerson, C., & Therrien, M. C. (2024). AAC & literacy: A scoping review of print knowledge measures for students who use aided augmentative and alternative communication. *Journal of Developmental and Physical Disabilities, 36*(4), 615–645.

Copeland, S. R., Keefe, E. B., & Luckasson, R. (2018). Literacy for all. In S. R. Copeland & E. B. Keefe (Eds.), *Effective literacy instruction for learners with complex support needs* (2nd ed., pp. 3–16). Paul H. Brookes Publishing Co.

De Valenzuela, J. S. (2018). Addressing cultural and linguistically diversity in language and literacy instruction. In S. R. Copeland & E. B. Keefe (Eds.), *Effective literacy instruction for learners with complex support needs* (2nd ed., pp. 21–34). Paul H. Brookes Publishing Co.

Ferrell, K. A., Bruce, S., & Luckner, J. L. (2014). Evidence-based practices for students with sensory impairments (Document No. IC-4). Retrieved from University of Florida, Collaboration for Effective Educator, Development, Accountability, and Reform Center website: http://ceedar.education.ufl.edu/tools/innovation-configurations/

Fisher, D., Flood, J., Lapp, D., & Frey, N. (2004). Interactive read alouds: Is there a common set of implementation practices. *The Reading Teacher, 58*(1), 8–17. https://doi.org/10.1598/RT.58.1.1

Giangreco, M. F., Shogren, K. A., & Dymond, S. K. (2020). Educating students with severe disabilities: Foundational concepts and practices. In F. Brown, J. McDonnell, & M.E. Snell (Eds.), *Instruction of students with severe disabilities: Meeting the needs of children and youth with intellectual disabilities, multiple disabilities, and autism spectrum disorders* (9th ed., pp. 1–27). Pearson.

Heller, K. W. (2017). Integrating health care in education programs. In F.P. Orelove, D. Sobsey, & D.L. Gilles (Eds.), *Educating students with severe and multiple disabilities: A collaborative approach* (5th ed., pp. 201–244). Paul H. Brookes Publishing Co.

Herzberg, T. S., Rosenblum, L. P., & Robbins, M. E. (2017). Teachers' experiences with literacy instruction for dual-media students who use print and braille. *Journal of Visual Impairments & Blindness, 111*(1), 49–59.

Hudson, M. (2020). Teaching English Language Arts standards across the grades. In D. M. Browder, F. Spooner, & G. R. Courtade (Eds.), *Teaching students with moderate and severe disabilities* (2nd ed., pp. 143–159). Guilford Press.

Llopart, M., & Esteban-Guitart, M. (2018). Funds of knowledge in 21st century societies: Inclusive educational practices for under-represented students. A literature review. *Journal of Curriculum Studies, 50*(2), 145–161.

Lim, N., O'Reilly, M. F., Sigafoos, J., Ledbetter-Cho, K., & Lancioni, G. E. (2019). Should heritage languages be incorporated into interventions for bilingual individuals with neurodevelopmental disorders? A systematic review. *Journal of Autism and Developmental Disorders, 49*, 887–912.

Luckner, J., Bruce, S., & Ferrell, K. A. (2016). A summary of communication and literacy evidence-based practices for students who are deaf and hard of hearing, visually impaired, and deafblind. *Communication Disorders Quarterly, 37*(4), 225–241. https://doi.org/10.1177/1525740115597507

McCarty, T., & Lee, T. (2014). Critical culturally sustaining/revitalizing pedagogy and Indigenous education sovereignty. *Harvard Educational Review, 84*(1), 101–124.

Mitchell, R. E., & Karchmer, M. A. (2004). Chasing the mythical ten percent: Parental hearing status of deaf and hard of hearing students in the United States. *Sign language studies, 4*(2), 138–163.

Murphy, K. A., Pentimont, J. M., & Chow, J. C. (2022). Supporting children's language and literacy through collaborative shared book reading. *Intervention in School and Clinic* 58, no. 3 (2023), 155–163.

National Reading Panel. (2000). Report of the National Reading Panel: Teaching children to read—An evidence-based assessment of the scientific research literature on reading and its implications for reading instruction (NIH Pub. No. 00–4769). Washington, DC: U.S. Department of Health and Human Services, Public Health Service, National Institute of Child Health and Human Development.

Niemiec, R. M., & Tomasulo, D. (2023). Introduction to disability and strengths-based approaches. In D. Tomasulo & R. M. Niemiec (Eds.), *Character Strengths and Abilities Within Disabilities: Advances in Science and Practice* (pp. 3–22). Springer International Publishing.

Ogletree, B. T., Wofford, M. C., & Barton-Hulsey, A. (2022). Practical approaches and socially valid assessment considerations for learners with emergent communication and severe intellectual disability. *Advances in Neurodevelopmental Disorders*, *6*(4), 426–441.

Ricketts, J., Jones, C. R. G., Happé, F., & Charman, T. (2013). Reading comprehension in autism spectrum disorders: The role of oral language and social functioning. *Journal of Autism and Developmental Disorders*, *43*(4), 807–816. https://doi.org/10.1007/s10803-012-1619-4

Ruppar, A. L. (2015). A preliminary study of the literacy experiences of adolescents with severe disabilities. *Remedial and Special Education*, *36*(4), 235–245.

Slowik, H. Y., and Brynelson, N. (2015). *Executive summary: English language arts/English language development framework for California public schools: Kindergarten through grade twelve*. Consortium for the Implementation of the Common Core State Standards.

Toews, S. G., McQuestion, J., & Kurth, J. A. (2021). Evaluation of the evidence base for shared reading to support literacy skill development for students with extensive support needs. *Research and Practice for Persons with Severe Disabilities*, *46*(2), 77–93.

Westling, D. L., Carter, E. W., Da Fonte, M. A., & Kurth, J. A. (2021). *Teaching students with severe disabilities*. Pearson.

White, J., McGarry, S., Falkmer, M., Scott, M., Williams, P. J., & Black, M. H. (2023). Creating inclusive schools for autistic students: A scoping review on elements contributing to strengths-based approaches. *Education Sciences*, *13*(7), 709.

Wofford, M. C., Ogletree, B. T., & De Nardo, T. (2022). Identity-focused practice in augmentative and alternative communication services: A framework to support the intersecting identities of individuals with severe disabilities. *American Journal of Speech - Language Pathology (Online)*, *31*(5), 1933–1948. https://doi.org/10.1044/2022_AJSLP-21-00397

Zebehazy K. T., & Wilton A. P. (2014). Quality, importance, and instruction: The perspectives of teachers of students with visual impairments on graphics use by students. *Journal of Visual Impairment & Blindness*, *108*, 5–16. https://doi.org/10.1177/0145482X1410800102

2

Communication Development for Learners with Extensive Support Needs

Individuals with extensive support needs are a heterogeneous group of learners who often have cognitive, physical, and sensory disabilities that result in complex communication needs and impact the development of symbolic communication (Erikson & Geist, 2016). Because of the variability from student to student, it can be challenging to support and integrate communication development consistently into instruction. This chapter will explore strategies for communication development, including augmentative and alternate communication (AAC), to support students with extensive support needs, including those who are English-language learners.

Communication Development

Communication is not only a basic life function but also a basic need that impacts all aspects of one's life (Brady et al., 2016). Learners with extensive support needs may have highly idiosyncratic or unique ways of expressing themselves that may or may not include verbal language. This can make it difficult for their communication attempts to be broadly recognized and understood, especially by someone new or within a new setting. To understand how to support learners with extensive support needs to further their communication abilities, it is important to first understand how our abilities to express ourselves and to understand incoming information develop and increase in complexity (Table 2.1).

TABLE 2.1 Levels of Communication Complexity

Communication Level	Definition		Example
Preintentional Behavior	Behavior is not under the individual's control but indicates their physiological state.		Exhibiting crying, facial expressions, and/or movements when hungry, tired, or hurt.
Intentional Behavior	Behavior is under the individual's control but not yet used to communicate.		Knocking over an object.
Presymbolic	Communicative behavior that does not involve any sort of symbol. It can be unconventional (not socially acceptable as we mature) or conventional (commonly used).		Unconventional body movements, vocalizations, facial expressions and simple gestures (such as tugging on people). Conventional pointing, nodding or shaking the head, waving, hugging, and looking from a person to a desired object.
Symbolic	Concrete Symbols	Symbols that look, feel, move, or sound like what they represent.	Pictures, objects (such as a shoelace to represent "shoe"), "iconic" gestures (such as patting a chair to say "sit down") and sounds (such as making a buzzing sound to mean "bee").
	Abstract Symbols	Symbols that are not similar to what they represent.	Speech, manual signs, line drawings, braille or printed text.

Adapted from Rowland and Schweigert (1989).

Communication development begins with preintentional behaviors, where the communicative behaviors are not within the individual's control but mirror their general state (hungry, tired, uncomfortable) and must be interpreted by a caregiver. This will eventually develop into intentional behaviors that are within the individual's control but are not yet used to communicate. Next to develop are presymbolic communication behaviors like body movements, gestures, or facial expressions that are intentionally used to communicate but do not involve the use of symbols. These behaviors begin as unconventional (intentional but not appropriate for an adult to use) and later progress into more conventional actions that are widely used by other individuals from the same culture. Eventually, symbolic communication develops, which includes the use of symbols that range in sophistication from concrete to abstract. Aside from the level of complexity, specific communication forms or methods of expression can be aided (pictures, line drawings, tactile representations) or unaided (gestures, speech, manual signs), with most individuals exhibiting communication that ranges in complexity and form. Expressive outputs (how an individual shares information) and receptive inputs (how an individual understands information presented to them) can also differ from one another in level of complexity and with the variety of forms used and understood (Brady et al., 2020).

Because of the communication challenges individuals with extensive support needs, especially those with deafblindness, often face, relationships with others can be significantly impacted. Social communication is the use of verbal and nonverbal communicative behaviors to interact with other individuals (Hansen et al., 2018; Dykstra et al., 2012). This includes communicative functions such as social interaction, behavior regulation, and joint attention. Social interaction includes the development of eye gaze (coordinated eye movements such as eye contact and gaze shifting) and imitation. Behavior regulation includes initiating a communicative behavior to gain access to an object, individual, or action. Lastly, joint attention (sharing attention with another person over an object) is connected to engagement. These skills typically develop in young children through play; however, individuals with extensive support needs often need to be explicitly taught these skills later in life. Limitations in social communication also impact the individual's literacy development, especially when joint attention skills have not been fully developed. Chapter three will provide a social communication assessment to support the integration of these critical skills into an interactive literacy activity.

Strategies for Supporting Communication Development During Literacy Instruction

Communication is an interactive and multidimensional process; thus, intervention for learners with extensive support needs goes beyond the interaction with their communication partner to also include the environment. When thinking about literacy instruction for learners with extensive support needs, including strategies that support communication development (Bruce & Bashinski, 2017), it can be reconceptualized for learners to maximize engagement and interaction for a variety of learners during literacy instruction.

Reflexive Partners

Communication and literacy are both interactive in nature. It is essential for a communication partner to be *reflexive* to support the learner's expressive communication throughout the activity, moving beyond simply understanding the learner's cues and communication modes towards interpreting their communicative initiations while also consistently responding and reinforcing communication attempts throughout the activity. This includes maintaining the expectation that the learner will communicate throughout the interaction, even when using unconventional forms. A reflexive communication partner must be familiar with the learner to be able to efficiently recognize the attempts and respond accordingly to reinforce the effort, which will increase the likelihood of more attempts and, eventually, spontaneous initiations. This also includes being sensitive to changes in the learner's overall attention, affect, and level of engagement.

During literacy activities, reflexive partners can enhance their responsiveness to the variety of communication forms the learner may utilize. Examples of presymbolic communication forms may include body language, like turning away as a means of saying "no" or using eye gaze to look at a desired item. Examples of symbolic communication include picture cards to identify characters from the story or objects that can be used to replicate an action from the text. Throughout the activity, the partner can make adjustments accordingly to sustain the interaction based on the learner's emotional state, alertness, and responses.

Collaboration with related service personnel may help to identify the communication needs and attempts of the individual. For example, physical and occupational therapists can help position and identify the difference between intentional and unintentional movements, while a speech-language pathologist (SLP) can support the identification of the learner's intentional communication attempts and assist the communication partner in developing consistent responses to the learner's initiations.

Consistency

Activities with a predictable structure and implementation sequence allow a learner with extensive support needs to develop their receptive communication. Routines, especially within-activity routines, can provide frequent opportunities to practice skills when communication partners thoughtfully embed repetitive opportunities throughout the activity. Increasing learner familiarity with the parts of an activity supports the establishment of predictability, anticipation, and an overall sense of security. One way to ensure consistency with a communication intervention is to embed it within activities to ensure frequent and consistent practice. Integrating communication development efforts into well-established routines requires determining the steps of the activity and identifying logical opportunities for the learner to communicate expressively. It is important to remember that routines cycle through initiation, preparation, activity, and termination phases. Communication opportunities can be interlaced throughout each phase of a routine to ensure ongoing participation.

Literacy interactions, such as shared book reading, can be structured so that multiple opportunities for communication can occur throughout the activity. For the learner who utilizes nonsymbolic communication, a routine can be established by maintaining a consistent sequence of actions each time you read a book together. For example, allowing the student to make a choice between two books, touching the title and exploring the cover, pausing after a page is read to explore the pictures, turning the pages together, and then returning the book to its shelf after reading to terminate the activity. A within-activity schedule can be used to support a learner who communicates symbolically. This includes providing representation for each action associated with the activity organized in a linear fashion. For example, photographs can be used to represent each of the actions associated with reading (selecting a book, pointing to the title, turning each page, and returning the book when finished). The representations selected to identify each step should be carefully selected based on the student's assessed level of symbolic understanding (see Chapter 3). Similar to a within-activity schedule, a sequence board (left-to-right symbol display) with objects related to the story can be used during interactive reading that corresponds to the sequence of the story.

Team members can be integral to the successful implementation of a structured and consistent literacy activity. Literacy supports, such as text or photo labels, can be integrated into the learning environment and consistently referenced throughout the day, for example, by touching a tactile marker before entering a room. With the support of the teacher of the blind and visually impaired (TVI), braille labels, textures, or even objects can be added to enhance the accessibility of each label and support their relevance to a broader range of students. Additionally, a teacher of the deaf and hard of hearing (TOD) can ensure the student has optimal access to auditory information and proper language supports are in place. Routines can also be extended outside of the classroom; for example, a within-activity routine can be used during small group sessions led by the SLP or sent home for a parent to use during bedtime reading.

Integrating Opportunities
Communication development for learners with extensive support needs goes beyond simply understanding when the learner

is attempting to communicate. Communication partners must consistently integrate meaningful opportunities for the learner to communicate throughout the activity to increase the rate and intention of the learner's communication. This also will support the development of joint attention, where the learner and adult are attending to and interacting during the activity together. Once an activity routine has been well-established, multiple opportunities for communication between the learner and communication can be embedded at set points. These opportunities focus on eliciting expressive output from the learner. Consider embedding opportunities for the individual to initiate a request, demonstrate refusal, or a combination, like demonstrating anticipation and a request. Incorporating periodic opportunities for choice-making and encouraging turn-taking can support an ongoing communicative interaction between the learner and the communication partner. Also, intentionally disrupting the activity routine by removing a familiar step and utilizing **wait time** can be an effective strategy to elicit spontaneous expressive output.

When planning a literacy lesson, structure opportunities to engage the student in communication before, during, and after reading. Choice-making opportunities can include having the student select the book to be read, allowing the student to choose which student in the small group will read the next page, or providing a choice of picture cards after reading to answer comprehension questions. Turn-taking is an easy strategy to incorporate during reading, which may include

> **WAIT TIME** is a critical component of this strategy and allows the learner additional time to process what is being asked of them and formulate a response. Establishing a consistent amount of time for each individual has been proven to be an effective way of increasing communication output for learners with extensive support needs and includes a set amount of time (3, 5, 10, or 15 seconds, depending on the learner) as well as maintaining a connection with the learner to let them know you are waiting. This may include maintaining eye contact, physical proximity, or touch (if the learner has a visual impairment). Lastly, wait time may also need to be extended if the individual requires additional time to access an AAC device. For example, in addition to the time needed to process the question, the individual needs time to scan the response options on the device and elicit the physical action to select the correct icon or area to produce the response.

sharing opportunities with the student to activate a switch to play a repeated line of text from the story or sharing interactions with the physical book, such as turning pages and pointing to pictures to find the main character(s). When thinking about disrupting the activity routine to encourage expressive output from the student, failing to advance to the next page while reading can provide a natural opportunity for the student to potentially initiate the action, ask for assistance, or expressively indicate that the routine was disrupted and the activity needs to continue.

Integrating communication opportunities throughout the literacy activity is a way to maintain the learner's attention and engagement throughout the activity. Support from physical and occupational therapists may be necessary to ensure optimal positioning so that the individual can physically and visually access the book. The TVI can support the structure of the lesson with information on the ideal proximity to the book the learner requires, as well as any communication needs to ensure optimal access. Additionally, the SLP can support the integration of AAC technology into the activity, program speech-generating devices, and directly support the student to activate the device during the activity.

Environmental Regulation

The environment plays a critical role in supporting communication development for learners with extensive support needs. This includes natural contexts that the learner frequents and encompasses the communication partner, peers, and activity. Throughout the activity, this strategy focuses on monitoring how environmental stimulus is impacting the learner. Automatic physical and neurological responses to environmental stimuli can impact the learner's readiness to engage in a communicative interaction. Consider the simultaneous sensory information the learner is receiving from their visual (seeing), auditory (hearing), tactile (touching), olfactory (smelling), and gustatory (tasting) channels throughout the activity, understanding that input may shift, with stimulus increasing or decreasing periodically. Regulating the environment includes ambient considerations, such as overhead and natural lighting, background noise, temperature, movement, and smells from food preparation around meal times. Regulating the environment for communication also includes orienting and varying movement and positioning depending on the ambient sensory input present at that time.

When planning a literacy activity, it is important to consider ambient sensory stimulation not only together but also individually. For example, laminating materials can increase their durability; however, depending on the lighting in the environment (natural and electric), it can also cause glare and limit the learner's visual access to the material. Background music, fans, side conversations, and passing hallway sounds can add additional auditory input into the environment that may make it difficult for the learner to maintain joint attention during the activity. Similarly, visual clutter on walls, the amount of movement within the immediate space, and the proximity of others (near or far) can impact the learner's participation in the communicative interactions planned throughout the activity. Adjustments to the environment to support the learner's attention and engagement can include removing distracting stimuli, altering the learner's positioning arrangement, altering the immediate location of the activity, or shifting the time of day that the activity occurs.

Environmental regulation can be supported by a range of related service professionals to maximize student participation and use of their sensory channels. When considering sensory input within the environment, TVIs can functionally assess the activity arrangement and location for factors that may impact visual access, such as glare, and suggest changes to set-up and materials as needed. This also includes ensuring text is enlarged at an appropriate size and that items, such as a slant board, are utilized to properly position the text within the student's field of vision. Similarly, a TOD can evaluate ambient noise and suggest amplification supports or changes in seating or positioning to optimize the learner's auditory access. Additionally, a certified orientation and mobility specialist can support movement and physical engagement throughout the activity and identify necessary accommodations that a learner who is blind or visually impaired may require to meaningfully and safely participate in the activity.

Pairing Communication Forms

Many individuals learn to communicate in specific ways by imitating the communication happening around them. By modeling multiple communication forms simultaneously, a communication partner can support the receptive communication development of the learner with extensive support needs. This can be as simple as a communication partner pairing two communication forms together, such as speech and ASL, to support the learner's understanding of the message being conveyed. When considering which communication forms to use with a learner, it is important to consider the level of complexity. Some symbols can serve as concrete and symbolic representations. For example, a photograph of the actual item it represents is concrete (e.g., a water bottle); however, if that photograph is used to represent all water bottles or "drink," it then becomes abstract. Pairing multiple forms does not always have to include active input from a communication partner using speech. For instance, adding a photograph to a speech-generating device is a way to passively pair forms to support receptive communication development. Movement and objects, in the form of gestures and object representations, can also be an effective way to pair communication forms. Gestures can support presymbolic and symbolic communication and can take a variety of forms, such as a nod paired with a verbal "yes," demonstrating how an object is used, or a palm-up with flexing fingers gesture paired with the phrase "come with me." Object representations (see the Tangible Symbols section below) include entire or partial objects that are used to represent nouns, verbs, emotions, positions, directions, etc. A strong connection must be maintained with the item or action it represents, and, often, learners will need to be taught the meaning of an object representation. Object representations are also presented below as they relate to students with visual impairments.

Pairing communication forms during literacy activities can be an effective way of supporting receptive language throughout the activity. This can be accomplished in a variety of ways, depending on the forms understood by the learner. Speech can be paired with actions, such as labeling book handling actions (e.g., "Let's turn the page"), and can include object representations that connect to characters or actions within the book being read. Here, multiple forms (speech, text, object) can be paired before reading as an introduction, during reading to augment the text, and after reading to measure comprehension. To effectively build vocabulary and comprehension, it is vital to maintain consistency with the names of items and with what they represent.

Support on pairing communication forms will mainly be received from the SLP and TVI. The SLP can guide the consideration of different communication to be included within the activity, identifying a combination that is best suited for the learner and their communication needs. The TVI can support the effort by ensuring that the symbolic representations used are visually accessible to the student while also supporting the development of object representations and material access. This includes ensuring the font is correctly sized, background contrast is optimal, and textures and/or braille labels are added as needed to support understanding. Additionally, support can also be received from the TOD, who may be able to direct how auditory forms should be used with the learner.

Students with Sensory Impairments

For individuals with visual impairment, hearing loss, or deafblindness, meaning-making during literacy engagement is often grounded in experience (Bruce & Brum, 2025). Because of the interconnectedness of language and literacy, sensory impairments may impact the learner's access to and engagement with the content.

Students with visual impairments benefit from early exposure to print and braille through meaningful interactions that can support their preference for either modality (Ferrell et al., 2014). For example, for students who will access literacy through print, early instruction on using low-vision devices and/or magnifying equipment can improve overall access to print, while early intensive and structured braille instruction can lead to increased fluency and comprehension. When considering modalities such as print or braille, it is essential to consult with a TVI familiar with the student.

When considering supporting students who are deaf or hard of hearing, it is important to consider the student's primary language. Spoken English has a clear connection to print; however, the unique vocabulary and language structure of American Sign Language (ASL), which does not parallel spoken or written English, can cause a disconnect for learners. Communication and literacy support for learners who are deaf or hard of hearing will depend on the individual's level of functional hearing. For students with functional hearing, literacy instruction should focus on phonemic awareness, phonics, fluency, vocabulary, and comprehension, whereas for students with limited functional hearing, visual representation, such as the use of fingerspelling connected with printed letters, can support the understanding of symbols and their meanings (Ferrell et al., 2014). Consulting with an audiologist and/or certified TOD can support the development of communication supports to implement during instruction.

As mentioned previously, the implications of deafblindness are compounded, and are more complex then simply adding the implications of the vision impairment to those associated with hearing loss. Rather, the result is a unique set of implications. Literacy for learners who are deafblind centers on interactive, hands-on experiences with representations, with a deep connection to the learner's communication development. Because opportunities for incidental learning are greatly impacted by deafblindness, most often information and concepts must be explicitly taught through multiple sensory channels, including sometimes using vision, hearing, and touch simultaneously. Many learners who are deafblind have some levels of residual vision or hearing, and it is important to consult with relevant related service supports (TVI, TOD, SLP) when selecting modalities for instruction.

Augmentative and Alternative Communication

The American Speech-Language-Hearing Association (2024) defines Augmentative and Alternative Communication, or AAC, as ways to communicate that supplement or compensate for their communication abilities. This includes spoken, written, and manual forms of communication. AAC can be unaided, such as communication through gestures, facial expressions, and manual signs, or aided, which requires additional items such as a communication board (with pictures, objects, line drawings, etc.), tablet, or other speech-generating device. AAC can also be classified as low-tech (e.g., communication book or alphabet display), mid-tech (e.g., single button device or overlay display, such as a Big Mack GoTalk), or high-tech (e.g., tablet, such as an ipad). Regardless of the complexity of the system used, the user must be taught how to use AAC to authentically incorporate it into their communication repertoire (Ivy et al., 2020). There are pros and cons to both unaided and aided AAC, and it is important to collaborate with families and a SLP before selecting an AAC system for a learner with extensive support needs.

Tangible Symbols

For learners with extensive support needs who also experience visual impairments or deafblindness, tangible symbols are a form of communication that uses whole or partial objects to represent a referent or a person, place, thing, activity, or concept that is being represented (Trief et al., 2009). They are meant to be handled and manipulated by the learner and have a connection to the referent. Tangible symbols reduce the cognitive demand and can serve as a bridge for learners to progress towards more abstract communication forms. The symbols are usually individualized for specific learners; however, there is some consistency among the tangible symbols frequently used in schools. Table 2.2 provides a limited list of tangible symbols. The objects used to create the tangible can be mounted or unmounted and can include a label with print and/or braille. Tangible symbols become more abstract as the symbol distances or bears less resemblance to the

TABLE 2.2 Universal Tangible Symbols

Referent (Activity)	Tangible Symbol
Literacy or Reading	Small book
Art	Crayon or paintbrush
Nap time	Small cut out from a blanket
Drink	Cup
Bubbles	Bubble wand
Car ride	Car key

Adapted from Trief et al. (2009).

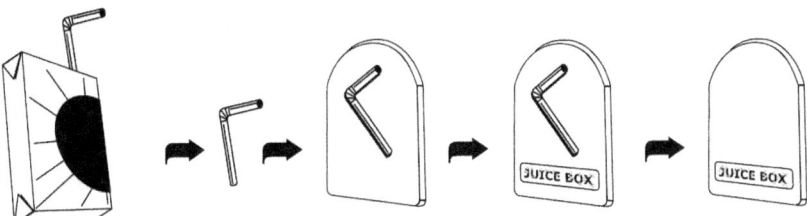

FIGURE 2.1 Hierarchy of abstraction for students who are learning to use tactile symbols

referent (see Figure 2.1). Initially, the object is not mounted, so the individual can fully tactually explore the object. Once mounted, the object is tactually different.

FIGURE 2.2 Example of a mounted tangible symbol representing "reading" as an activity

Tangible symbols are a form of graphic communication that can represent a variety of concepts. Whole objects can be used independently or mounted to a plastic card as a backing. Figure 2.2 is an example of a tangible symbol used to represent a reading activity. The object, a small book, is mounted to a plastic card and contains a text label that also includes a clear braille label over the word.

The shape of the plastic card can also be used to represent concepts that supplement the mounted object and label. Figure 2.3 provides examples of five plastic cards in different colors and shapes that are used to represent wh- questions. These cards can then be sequenced to tell a story.

FIGURE 2.3 Sequence cards for telling a story

Strategies for Implementing AAC

When planning to implement an AAC system, it is important to remember that most individuals use a combination of unaided (natural communication from the body) and aided (supported with an external tool) AAC to supplement their communication (Reichle et al., 2019). This section will focus on integrating an AAC system into a literacy lesson.

Step 1: Evaluate the Activity and Environment

Before even considering which type of AAC system to implement, it is important to understand the expectations for the student during the activity related to communication, participation, and physical movement and access. This can happen formally by conducting an ecological inventory or informally by systematically reviewing the activity and the expectations for student engagement and participation. For an interactive reading lesson, is the expectation that the student will respond to questions using specific information or vocabulary from the text, or will questions be presented that lend to more general responses? Will this expectation change throughout the activity when the focus changes from answering comprehension questions to sequencing events from the plot? To best evaluate the communication and participation expectations of the activity, think about how a grade-level peer might participate in the activity. This will allow the learner with extensive support needs to receive support that will maximize their participation and engagement in the activity.

Step 2: Evaluate Communication Modes

It is important to select communication modes that are accessible to the learner and align with their level of symbolic understanding (see Table 2.1). When integrating AAC supports into a literacy activity, the modes can be aided or unaided and range in complexity. Consider teaching new communication forms using modality sampling. The process begins with systematic observation of the learner interacting with preferred communication partners to identify their commonly used communication forms. The learner is then taught a novel symbol across three types of

AAC (vocal, as well as unaided and aided AAC). This provides information on which forms are easily learned, sustained, and possibly generalized by the individual.

Step 3: Selecting Communication Forms
With the results of the modality sampling in Step 2 and the environmental assessment in Step 1, communication forms can be identified that align with the communicative demands of the literacy lesson. Based on the learner's level of communication complexity, concrete or abstract representations may be used that include gestures, tangible symbols, photos, line drawings, text, or manual signs. Note that different modes may be used at different times during the activity. For example, the student may be expected to provide a yes/no response verbally or using an unaided gesture, like a head nod or shake, whereas for other parts of the activity, say sequencing events from the text, the student will rely on aided means, like picture cards or a speech-generating device. Before selecting specific symbols, it is recommended to create a list of the identified communication modes paired with the forms selected that are aligned with each part of the activity.

Step 4: Creating Aided Representations
When considering creating individual representations that align with the identified communication form (tangible symbols, photos, line drawings, text, or manual signs) that will serve as aided AAC supports during an interactive literacy activity, consider the vocabulary that is going to be represented. The representation can signify a broader category (e.g., fruit) or a very specific item (e.g., banana). Consider its generalizability and if the goal is to encourage the student to use the representation outside of the literacy lesson. Consult with the SLP on the benefits of incorporating core vocabulary (common pronouns, verbs, descriptors, and question words) as a part of the lesson or on the learner's device or communication board. When creating representations for learners who have visual impairments or deafblindness, avoid using miniatures, as they hold no meaning if the individual cannot see the larger item in its entirety but rather experience it in pieces.

For example, for a learner who is blind, a piece of a seatbelt is a better referent to a car than a matchbox car because the seatbelt is part of the experience of riding in a car and is something the individual can touch, experience, and use. Labels on the representation (text, braille, or both) can be helpful to simultaneously expose learners to more abstract representations and also support consistent naming by staff and students. When using text labels, be sure the size is appropriate for the learner's visual abilities.

Conclusion

Here are some points to consider when thinking about communication development for learners with extensive support needs:

- Understand *HOW* the learner communicates. Assessment is essential to gain an understanding of the specific forms and modes the learner uses to communicate.
- Learners with extensive support needs may simultaneously use a variety of communication forms. It is essential for the communication partner to attune to the learner's expressive communication outputs, even if they are very subtle.
- Collaborate with the multidisciplinary team to integrate communication opportunities throughout daily activities so that learners with extensive support needs have multiple authentic opportunities to interact with others as they build their communication skills. This can also support sustained attention and engagement throughout the day.
- AAC systems can open an entire world of communication for a learner with extensive support needs that use nonverbal means of expression. Consult and work together with the learner's SLP to develop an AAC system that can be used across home and school settings. Consider representations, such as tangible symbols, that combine multiple communication forms and can be integrated into the classroom environment.

References

American Speech-Language-Hearing Association. (2005). Augmentative and Alternative Communication (AAC) [Website]. Available from https://www.asha.org/njc/aac/.

Brady, N. C., Bruce, S., Goldman, A., Erickson, K., Mineo, B., Ogletree, B. T., Paul, D., Romski, M. A., Sevcik, R., Siegel, E., Schoonover, J., Snell, M., Sylvester, L., & Wilkinson, K. (2016). Communication services and supports for individuals with severe disabilities: guidance for assessment and intervention. *American Journal on Intellectual and Developmental Disabilities, 121*(2), 121–138. https://doi.org/10.1352/1944-7558-121.2.121

Brady, N. C., Romine, R. E. S., Holbrook, A., Fleming, K. K., & Kasari, C. (2020). Measuring change in the communication skills of children with autism spectrum disorder using the communication complexity scale. *American Journal on Intellectual and Developmental Disabilities, 125*(6), 481–492.

Bruce, S. M., & Bashinski, S. M. (2017). The trifocus framework and interprofessional collaborative practice in severe disabilities. *American Journal of Speech-Language Pathology, 26*(2), 162–180.

Bruce, S., & Brum, C. (2025). Emergent literacy in individuals who are deafblind. In T. Hartshorne, M. J. Janssen, & W. Wittich (Eds.), *Volume II: Learning, education and support of deafblind children and adults: An interdisciplinary approach. Series: Perspectives in deafness.* Oxford University Press.

Dykstra, J. R., Boyd, B. A., Watson, L. R., Crais, E. R., & Baranek, G. T. (2012). The impact of the Advancing Social-communication And Play (ASAP) intervention on preschoolers with autism spectrum disorder. *Autism, 16*(1), 27–44.

Erickson, K. A., & Geist, L. A. (2016). The profiles of students with significant cognitive disabilities and complex communication needs. *Augmentative and Alternative Communication* (Baltimore, Md. : 1985), *32*, 187–197. https://doi.org/10.1080/07434618.2016.1213312

Ferrell, K. A., Bruce, S., & Luckner, J. L. (2014). Evidence-based practices for students with sensory impairments (Document No. IC-4). Retrieved from University of Florida, Collaboration for Effective Educator, Development, Accountability, and Reform Center website: http://ceedar.education.ufl.edu/tools/innovation-configurations/

Hansen, S. G., Carnett, A., & Tullis, C. A. (2018). Defining early social communication skills: A systematic review and analysis. *Advances in Neurodevelopmental Disorders, 2*, 116–128.

Ivy, S., Robbins, A., & Kerr, M. G. (2020). Adapted Picture Exchange Communication System using tangible symbols for young learners with significant multiple disabilities. *Augmentative and Alternative Communication, 36*(3), 166–178. https://doi.org/10.1080/07434618.2020.1826051

Reichle, J., Simacek, J., Wattanawongwan, S., & Ganz, J. (2019). Implementing aided augmentative communication systems with persons having complex communicative needs. *Behavior Modification, 43*(6), 841–878.

Rowland, C., & Schweigert, P. (1989). Tangible symbols: Symbolic communication for individuals with multisensory impairments. *Augmentative and Alternative Communication, 5*, 226–234. https://doi.org/10.1080/07434618912331275276

Trief, E., Bruce, S. M., Cascella, P. W., & Ivy, S. (2009). The development of a universal tangible symbol system. *Journal of Visual Impairment & Blindness, 103*(7), 425-430.

3

Assessment for Learners with Extensive Support Needs

Assessment is the starting place for all instruction, as it is impossible to know where to begin teaching without an understanding of what the student can accomplish independently or with some support. This chapter will guide you through the assessment of literacy and communication skills. This includes important considerations that can impact a student's ability to demonstrate their skills, as well as conducting baseline and summative measures before and after instruction to support the development of learning goals and to understand the skills that have been acquired. Chapter 6 will cover formative assessment that you will use during interactive reading to improve your teaching and provide ongoing feedback to your students.

Assessment Considerations for Individuals with Extensive Support Needs

Because of the heterogeneous nature of the population, there is no "one-size-fits-all" assessment for individuals with extensive support needs. When identifying academic learning goals, teachers must consider functional academic skills as well as areas of participation in the general education curriculum (Westling et al., 2021). This includes considering the student's baseline skill level, the overall academic skill, state curriculum standards, and curricular benchmarks to generate an appropriate learning goal for the student (Niemiec & Tomasulo, 2023). When considering applying this to literacy skill acquisition, think about the overall goal you have identified for the students, as well as the individual, or discreet, behaviors that contribute to or make up the larger goal. For example, if the overall literacy goal for a student is to increase their participation in an interactive reading activity, think about the observable behaviors that constitute "participating" for that student, understanding that this may differ from student to student.

When developing assessments for learners with limited communication skills, such as those with extensive support needs, there are many factors to consider. For example, administration by a familiar adult, environment, and location, identifying signs of distress, and length of time (Clendon et al., 2021). Additionally, identifying how the individual will respond is also critical, especially for learners who utilize unconventional means of communication. When considering the assessment of literacy skills, it is important to include both formal and informal assessments, as well as obtain a comprehensive measure of the learner's emergent and conventional literacy skills before developing learning goals and intervention targets (McIntyre et al., 2022).

The comprehensive approach to assessment includes specific considerations for learners with extensive support needs, including attention to their preferred methods of communication and sensory channels. Integrating the key characteristics of individuals with extensive support needs related to learning and abilities, social abilities, and physical characteristics (Westling et al., 2021) with the skills associated with emergent and conventional literacy (Clendon et al., 2021) can provide a comprehensive baseline understanding of a student's abilities as well as support the identification of appropriate learning targets for interactive literacy instruction. Additionally, the assessment of social-communication skills can ensure the integration of communication development within the literacy activity (Watson et al., 2011).

TABLE 3.1 Sample Interest Inventory for Learners with Extensive Support Needs

Student Name:	Date:

Directions: Interview someone familiar with the individual to obtain an understanding of their interests and preferences.
(1) Can you provide me with some background information on [name]?   (2) How does [name] communicate with you? Do they speak or understand other languages?   (3) What aspects of your home culture and/or language is [name] particularly drawn to? For example, certain holiday, books, songs, activities, etc.?   (4) In general, what are some of the things [name] is interested in? Are there certain things they get excited about?   (5) What are [name]'s favorite activities?   (6) Do they have any favorite books and/or authors?   (7) Are there activities that [name] enjoys doing with you or someone else?   (8) Does [name] have any talents?   (9) What are some of the things that [name] dislikes?   (10) Is there anything else about [name] that you would like to share?
Please circle areas of interests: Animals   Dates   Mechanical   Plants   Sports   Art   Geology   Music   Politics   Things   Astronomy   History   Numbers   Psychology   Time   Collections   Machines   Objects   Reading   Toys   Computers   Maps   People   Religion   Transportation   Construction   Math   Physics   Schedules   TV
Additional information to include:

Comprehensive assessment across various domains can provide a holistic understanding of how a student with extensive support needs is functioning and support teachers to authentically plan an interactive literacy activity that is meaningful, engaging, and targets relevant communication and literacy skills. The following section will describe the various domains that can impact a student's access to instruction and Table 3.2 will provide a list of assessment resources for each domain.

Personal Characteristics

Understanding the personal characteristics of the learner with extensive support needs will not only identify potential support to implement during an activity to increase engagement and participation but also describe the unique implications of their disability. When assessing the learner's personal characteristics, one must consider the following areas:

- **Background information:** Etiology, diagnosis, age of onset, medical history, alertness, and current health status
- **Sensory Abilities:** Functional vision and hearing, specifically level of acuity, field of vision, perception, and tactile skills
- **Motor abilities:** Range of motion, strength, tone, positioning, and extent of voluntary control
- **Preferences and Interests:** Preferences and interests that can be used to motivate the learner's engagement and participation

Students with Sensory Impairment

A teacher of students who are blind or visually impaired (TVI) or certified orientation and mobility specialist (COMS) can provide essential support during the assessment process to ensure the student has proper access to the assessment activities and potential environmental barriers are mitigated. Similarly, for students who are deaf or hard of hearing, an audiologist or teacher of the deaf and hard of hearing (TOD) can be a vital resource to ensure auditory access throughout the assessment process and instruction. For learners who are deafblind, specific services depend on the individual's level of residual vision and hearing and may include a combination of services, including an intervener, who is a paraprofessional with specific training in deafblindness. The following section will detail specific assessments for students with sensory impairment.

Functional Vision and Learning Media Assessment
A Functional Vision and Learning Media Assessment, or FVLMA, is a structured assessment tool that combines the Functional Vision Assessment (FVA) and the Learning Media

Assessment (LMA). The FVLMA provides a framework for assessing visual functioning, identifying areas of need, and necessary adaptations of educational media.

Functional Vision Assessment

The FVA uses information from student records, teacher input, and observation to provide a better understanding of how the individual uses the vision they have in a variety of settings (REF). The purpose of an FVA can then be understood as obtaining an understanding of how the student sees things. This includes the behaviors they currently utilize to see and will result in suggested strategies to maximize their vision. An FVA must be conducted by a certified TVI or COMS specialist and typically begins with a review of records, such as eye reports (visual field, acuity, eye motility/movement, and diagnosis). The specific areas covered include acuity (clarity of near and distant vision), visual field, color, contrast sensitivity, eye movement (eye motility together and separately), motor behavior (visual and ocular), and perception (depth and visual). For students with extensive support needs, these areas are often assessed across environments and require prior collaboration with the classroom teacher and speech-language pathologist to ensure the necessary communication supports are in place. Specific behaviors that are observed during the assessment relate to how the learner positions their head/body when looking at people, objects/materials, optimal lighting (dim vs. bright), the onset of visual fatigue, preferred level of contrast for pictures and print, visual crowding (i.e., simplified vs. complex pictures or graphics), and the amount of distance a learner requires to see an item or printed material.

Learning Media Assessment

The Learning Media Assessment, or LMA, is a tool used to support practitioners in identifying the best learning mode (visual, auditory, tactile, kinesthetic, or olfactory) for a student with a visual impairment (Koeing & Holbrook, 1995). This comprehensive assessment utilizes information obtained from the FVA to identify appropriate sensory learning channels, reading readiness, and preferences during academic and functional activities across home and school settings to identify the learning modes the student regularly utilizes. The assessment begins with the TVI observing how the students receptively utilize their sensory channels with familiar locations across visual, auditory, tactile, olfactory, gustatory, and kinesthetic sensory channels and whether these channels were utilized spontaneously or required prompting. Once preferred channels have been identified, the assessment examines the student's readiness for literacy instruction, which can also include a supplementary measure of braille readiness using the Assessment of Braille Literacy Skills (ABLS).

Tactile Skills Assessment

An assessment of tactile skills, or haptic perception, can provide highly useful information on how students with visual impairment or who are deafblind receive information through their sense of touch. This includes obtaining information on how the individual explores, discriminates, and gathers information about their environment using one or both hands (Adkins et al., 2021). A thorough understanding of how the student receives information through touch can influence their ability to discriminate between two-dimensional items, such as raised graphics, as well as handle three-dimensional objects like tangible symbols, as described in the previous chapter. Tactile assessment is ultimately exploring the student's ability to use their hands; responsiveness to touch/vibration; exploring behaviors, such as reaching; object exploring, recognition, and handling; physical interactions; ability to recognize objects and people through touch; and their tolerance for physical demonstration using hand-over-hand and hand-under-hand techniques.

Informal Functional Hearing Evaluation

Through a collaborative team approach, the Informal Functional Hearing Evaluation (IFHE) is intended to determine how a student's hearing loss is impacting their learning and also support teams in identifying the appropriate accommodations and modifications to improve access and outcomes for the student (Montgomery & Graves, 2017). The IFHE can be used to describe how the student uses their hearing across settings and provide useful information on specific strategies to support students with hearing loss, as well as those who are deafblind. Information to complete the IFHE is gathered from parents and familiar practitioners on how the student utilizes their heading across settings and during different activities, as well as through natural and systematic observations that include integrating information from formal hearing evaluations to identify patterns and trends regarding the student's use of their hearing abilities. The process concludes with recommendations for accommodations and instructional strategies to improve the student's use of their functional hearing.

Communication Assessment

Authentic communication assessment for individuals with extensive support needs involves describing the individual's expressive and receptive communication abilities, the communication support they require across environments that they frequent, and the expectations of their familiar communication partners (Brady et al., 2016). It is important to remember that expressive and receptive forms can vary. Chapter 2 provides detailed information on supporting the communication abilities of students with extensive support needs, including AAC and tangible symbols. When planning an informal communication assessment, be sure to consider all four aspects of communication – form, function, content, and context – to ensure you obtain a holistic understanding of how the individual is communicating (Bruce, 2010). The section will explore two assessments to support communication assessment for learners with extensive support needs. Table 3.2 will also include additional assessments that can provide effective measures of expressive and receptive communication abilities for this population of learners.

Communication Complexity Scale
The Communication Complexity Scale (CCS) is an assessment measure used to measure early expressive communication acts

TABLE 3.2 Assessment Resources

Name	Description	Resources
Assessment of Braille Literacy Skills (ABLS)	Measure of readiness and pre-braille literacy skills for students with visual impairment and additional disabilities.	www.pathstoliteracy.org/resource/braille-assessment-checklist/
Basic Reading Inventory	Assessment for basic reading ability, including decoding and fluency.	Johns (2005)
Communication Complexity Scale (CCS)	Assesses the complexity of early communication for learners with extensive support needs.	https://data.lsi.ku.edu/ccs/
Communication Matrix	Assessment of early communication functions across communication forms.	www.communicationmatrix.org
Functional Vision and Learning Media Assessment (FVLMA)	Assess how a student uses their vision through comprehensive observations in appropriate learning mode(s) for a learner across multiple sensory channels.	www.aph.org/product/fvlma-kit/
Informal Functional Hearing Evaluation (IFHE)	Identify the impact of a student's hearing loss on their educational programming.	www.nationaldb.org/media/doc/IFHEFunctionalEvaluation_ae.pdf
Early Tactile Skills Learning Profile	Observation checklist to develop a profile of tactile abilities of a learner with a visual impairment.	www.tsbvi.edu/wp-content/uploads/assets/documents/statewide-resources/early-tactile-learning-profile-combined-fillable.pdf

that look at the individual's interactions with objects, people, and events across presymbolic and emerging symbolic means (Brady et al., 2012). It is a valid and reliable measure for individuals with extensive support needs of all ages who have minimal verbal skills and can serve as an effective means to monitor progress over time (Brady et al., 2018a). During the assessment, the evaluator creates structured opportunities for the learner to spontaneously initiate a communication act during a designated coding interval. This section will explain the administration of the CCS to gain an understanding of the communication abilities of a student with extensive support needs to support the planning of an effective interactive literacy lesson.

Communication Complexity, Mode, and Functions

The CCS looks to capture communication modes and functions (see Chapter 2) across structured activities. Communication behaviors are identified and scored for complexity across a 12-point scale that reflects preintentional communication, such as acts directed towards an object, intentional presymbolic gestures, such as vocalizations that may be combined with gestures, and symbolic communication acts that may include the use of words, print, braille, manual signs, or line drawings (see Table 3.3). For symbolic communication, specific modes are also recorded, including speech, using a speech-generating device, graphic use (line drawings or pictures), manual sign, and a combination of modes. Intentional communication acts (scores six and greater) are also coded for communication functions that include behavior regulation (requests or protests), joint attention (comments or social greetings), response to questions (communication act after a question), or prompted/imitated/reading (communication that is imitated or in response to a prompt). Additionally, the communication partner is also indicated for each recorded communicative behavior.

TABLE 3.3 Levels of the Communication Complexity Scale

Communication Level	Score	Communication Act	Example
Preintentional	1	Alerting: a change in behavior or stopping a behavior	Turning away from the activity or no change in the individual's behavior
	2	Single orientation only – on an object, event or person	Change in facial expression or body/head movement
	3	Single orientation only + 1 other PCB	Staring at a toy and vocalizing
	4	Single orientation only + 2 or more PCBs	Staring at a toy vocalizing and pointing to the toy
	5	Dual orientation: shift in focus between a person and an object, between a person and an event using vision, body orientation, etc. (without PCB)	Looking up from toy to examiner
Intentional Non-symbolic	6	Triadic orientation (eye gaze or touch from object to person and back)	Looking from toy to examiner and back to toy within a short time frame
	7	Dual orientation + 1 PCB	Looking from toy to examiner and vocalizing
	8	Dual orientation + 2 or more PCBs	Looking from toy to examiner, vocalizing and pointing to toy
	9	Triadic orientation + 1 PCB	Looking from toy to examiner back to toy and vocalizing
	10	Triadic orientation + 2 or more PCBs	Looking from toy to examiner back to toy, vocalizing and waving at toy
Intentional Symbolic	11	One-word verbalization, sign, or AAC symbol selection	Selecting symbol for "ball" from a four-choice array
	12	Multi-word verbalization, sign, or AAC symbol selection	Saying "more ball" to request the ball

Note: PCB = potentially communicative behavior

Reproduced with permission from Brady et al. (2018b).

CCS Scoring

During a ten-minute observation, interval coding is used to identify the highest-scoring communication every 30 seconds, with a ten-second pause for documentation across 16 intervals. Only one communicative act can be scored per interval. Communication acts are documented using a score of 1–12. Recording sessions to be coded later are likely to improve the scorer's accuracy in the identification of communication acts. Scores can be analyzed by mode and/or function to aid with communication planning, goal development, and progress monitoring. Table 3.2 provides information on how to access the training modules and implementation guide for the CCS.

Communication Matrix

Similar to the CCS, the Communication Matrix assesses early communication functions (refuse, obtain, social, and information) across forms to chart the reasons and behaviors individuals use to communicate (Rowland, 2011). Available as a paper or an online tool, it organizes results into seven levels of communicative behavior: preintentional behavior, intentional behavior, unconventional presymbolic communication, conventional presymbolic communication, concrete symbols, abstract symbols, and language. It also allows individuals to demonstrate their communication skills through a variety of modes using presymbolic communication (gestures, body movements, vocalizations, eye gaze), abstract communication (braille, abstract and tangible symbols, pictures, writing, manual sign), and using speech-generating devices. The Communication Matrix also supports family input through a parent version of the assessment, and the results provide a clear visual to identify emerging and acquired skills, as well as to identify target skills and chart progress over time.

Assessment is an integral part of planning, implementing, and evaluating instruction, and there are certain factors that can support student success throughout the process to ensure an accurate understanding of their skill level is obtained. Assessments, whether formal or informal, should be conducted in a manner that is appropriate to the individual student and their needs. This includes physical, sensory, cognitive, and communication needs the student may have that, if not supported, can serve as a barrier to obtaining a true picture of their abilities. Table 3.4 provides specific domains to be assessed, as well as specific considerations for learners with extensive support needs.

TABLE 3.4 Assessment Considerations for Learners with Extensive Support Needs

Learner Characteristics

Domain	Description	Specific Considerations
Communication	Receptive	Are the assessment items and prompts provided to the leaner in a mode that is easily understood and accessible to the learner?
		Does the assessment include complex language, multi-step directives, or verbal only directions?
	Expressive	Can the learner express their responses to assessment items in a manner that is clear and easily understood by the assessor?
		Have accommodations been provided to allow the learner multiple means of response for assessment items?
	Social interactions	Will the learner initiate social interactions or respond to initiations?
		How does the learner respond to interactions with strangers?
		Is the assessor someone familiar to the learner?
	AAC	Is the learner's AAC device available during the assessment?
		Is the vocabulary available that is needed to accurately respond to assessment items?
	Distress	Is the assessor aware of the behaviors the learner demonstrates when in distress?

Learner Characteristics

Domain	Description	Specific Considerations
Physical	Upper and lower extremities	Does the assessment require movement from the upper extremities (e.g., using arms to manipulate items or physically navigating the environment)?
	Adaptive equipment	Has optimal position for each assessment activity been discussed? Does the learner have access during the assessment to the necessary adaptive equipment for positioning and/or mobility? Does certain equipment allow for ideal positioning? For example, using a prone stander may provide optimal trunk support for upper extremity mobility during a tabletop activity or the use of an adapted chair may provide additional support that will limit the need to cue the individual to "look" or "keep their head up" to visually access the materials.
Behavior	Self-stimulatory	Does the learner exhibit self-stimulatory behaviors that may impede their ability to participate in the assessment of that may be mistaken for an intentional communicative responsive?
	Self-injurious or harmful	Is the assessor familiar with the strategies to reduce or responses to undesired behaviors during the assessment? Does the assessment session(s) require an additional support person in the immediate area or someone on standby to intervene if needed?
Learning	Attention and alertness	How does the learner demonstrate that they are alert and attending to the assessor? How does the learner indicate a change in their level of attentiveness?
	Consistency	Is the learner consistent with their responses, including yes/no responses?

Learner Characteristics		
Domain	Description	Specific Considerations
Culture and Background	Culture and language Family life	Can familiar aspects of the learner's home culture be integrated into the assessment? Is someone in the learner's life more familiar with their current functioning and needs (e.g., primary caregiver)?
		Does the learner use a different language at home? Can the home language be integrated into the assessment?
	Medical history	Are there aspects of the learner's medical history that are relevant to the assessment sessions? For example, does the learner have a history of stress-induced seizures or do they require a medication at school that results in drowsiness?

Adapted from Bruce et al. (2016)

Foundational Literacy Skill Assessment

Foundational literacy skills include emergent literacy skills (print concepts, phonological awareness), phonics, word recognition, and fluency. Emergent literacy is often understood as the precursor to the traditional concept of literacy and includes skills, interactions, experiences, materials, and environments that lay the foundation for reading and writing print or braille (Nelson & Bruce, 2019). It is greater than a set of skills needed to read and write and includes the social interactions that happen around print within literacy-rich environments. The components of emergent literacy include language; conventions, purpose, and functions of print; knowledge of letters; phonological awareness, including linguistic awareness and phoneme-grapheme correspondence; emergent reading and writing; and print motivation (Gunn et al., 1995; Whitehurst & Lonigan, 1998). For advancing literacy skills, the National Reading Panel (2000) identified the "Five Pillars of Reading" (phonemic awareness, phonics, fluency, vocabulary, and comprehension) as the essential aspects of effective reading instruction.

Informal assessment of literacy skills can influence the development of learning goals and objectives for interactive reading. Table 3.5 provides an example of an informal foundational literacy skill assessment that can help obtain a baseline measure of an individual's literacy skills. This naturalistic form of assessment occurs during a typical interaction with a book and requires the adult partner to create situations for the student to demonstrate certain literacy behaviors. It is important to consider the different ways a particular student may respond and modify the assessment as needed to accommodate a specific student's communication abilities and support needs. The tool is organized by sections relating to book-handling skills, conventions of print, and phoneme-grapheme correspondence. A procedure for assessing each skill is suggested, which includes language for the assessor to utilize to encourage the demonstration of the specific skill. Behavior criteria are also included for each item, which may be useful when the demonstration of a particular item must be adapted to better align with a student's abilities. For example, the first item suggests placing a book with its front cover facing down to encourage the student to correctly orient it. However, the physical movement associated with this skill may not be possible for an individual with limited upper extremity movement abilities; thus, an adaptation could be to ask the student, "Is this the cover of the book?" or "Is this how we start with a book?" to see if they can identify that the orientation is not correct. Similarly, if using a switch to turn the pages of an electronic book is the most appropriate way for a particular learner to handle a book, then the assessment can be modified to reflect that student's specific way of accessing the content. Scoring for the assessment allows us to identify not only the accuracy of a student's response but also their level of independence.

> It is important to obtain a clear understanding of a student's abilities before developing instructional learning goals. The following tool can serve as a pre-and post-assessment to identify a student's emergent literacy skills. Each assessment item can be modified depending on a student's physical, sensory, or communication abilities.

TABLE 3.5 Foundational Literacy Skill Assessment Recording Sheet

Student Name:	Date:
Location:	Assessor:

Instructions: Ask the student the following questions to identify their emergent literacy skills. If necessary, allow students to respond in a variety of ways, including pointing, handing you an item, indicating yes/no, through eye-gaze, or using a speech-generating device.
Scoring for Accuracy (A): C = correct; X = incorrect; blank = no response   **Scoring for Independence (I):** P = prompt; I = Independent

Book Handling: Orienting a book correctly and identifying its parts			
Procedure	Criteria	A	I
[Place the book in front of the child incorrectly with upside down with back cover facing up] Assessor: *"Let's look at a book together."*	Correctly orients the book		
[Looking at the cover of the book] Assessor: *"This book is called [state title]. Where is the title?"*	Identifies the title		
[Looking at the cover of the book] Assessor: *"It was written by [state name of author]. Can you point to the author's name?"*	Identifies the author		
[After reading, pause and wait for student to turn the page.]	Turns a single page		

Conventions of print: Understanding of print, its structure, and how words convey meaning			
Procedure	Criteria	A	I
[Open to first page of story] Assessor: "Where do I start to read?"	Indicates the text		
[Open to a page of the text] Assessor: "Can you find a word?"	Identifies word on the page		
[Open to a page of the text] Assessor: "Can you follow along while I read?"	Moves finger left to right		
[Open to a page of the text] Assessor: "Where is the space between words?"	Identifies the space		
[Open to a page of the text] Assessor: "Where is the period/question mark?"	Identifies punctuation		

(Cont.)

TABLE 3.5 (Cont.)

[Open to a page of the text] Assessor: "Can you find a sentence for me?"	Identifies a sentence		
Phoneme-grapheme correspondence: Identifying letters and their corresponding sounds			
[Provide an assortment of letter tiles] Assessor: "Can you find the <letter name>?"	Letters identified:		
[Present student with a single letter tile] Assessor: "What sound does this make?"	Sounds identified:		
Word recognition and Fluency: Identifying words and the ability to read			
[Present the student with note cards containing high-frequency words] Assessor: "Which words do you see?"	Words identified:		
[Provide a passage of text to measure the individual's reading rate and level of accuracy for one minute] Assessor: "Can you read this passage to me?"	Words read correctly per minute (WCPM):		
Notes:			

Literacy-Rich Environments

Literacy-rich environments are an integral part of literacy development for all learners (Whitehurst & Lonigan, 1998). However, because of the specific needs of learners with extensive needs, learning environments can unintentionally become inaccessible, especially for learners with sensory impairments who may have greater sensitivity to certain stimuli or may require additional support to access their surroundings. When considering creating or modifying a learning environment to meet the needs of a variety of students, Universal Design for Learning (UDL) can serve as an effective framework to ensure access for everyone (Rose, 2000; https://udlguidelines.cast.org/). UDL looks to ensure that all learners have multiple means of engagement, representation, and action and expression to ensure meaningful participation in

> UDL can serve as an effective framework to ensure literacy-rich environments are accessible to all learners, including those with extensive support needs, including sensory impairments. Below are some considerations related to the environment and materials to support access for all learners.

learning. When used to evaluate a learning environment, UDL can support the development of a literacy-rich environment. Table 3.6 provides an ecological assessment that integrates the principles of UDL to assess the literacy learning environment for learners with extensive support needs.

Student Interest

The interests and preferences of learners with extensive support needs can serve as an effective means of maintaining interest and engagement in a learning activity (Bruce et al., 2024). An ecological approach can be used to gain information regarding preferences, community engagement, home life, and prior experiences (Ryndak et al., 2020). Information can be obtained from the individual, their grade-level peers, families, educators, or related service personnel. Eliciting parent involvement through interviews, home visits, telling stories, and parent nights can be an effective means of learning about a student's interests and preferences while also supporting culturally sustaining pedagogy (Goodman & Hooks, 2016). Additionally, utilizing a list of special interests can also serve as an effective starting place to identify areas of interest (Nowell et al., 2021). Table 3.1 provides an example of an informal interest inventory to use with families and other people familiar with the learner who has extensive support needs.

Professional Collaboration

Because of the complex nature of individuals with extensive support needs, it is recommended to invite members of

TABLE 3.6 Considerations for Evaluation of the Literacy Environment

		Yes	No
Learning Environment	Students are able to easily get to the learning area, including those using mobility and positioning equipment such as wheelchairs, walkers, adapted seating, and/or prone/supine standers.		
	Walkways are clear as well as free from clutter and obstacles.		
	Each student has a designated area to work that allows them to complete the instructional tasks.		
	Materials are organized, labeled, and can be accessed by students (or easily made accessible) and returned to a designated location after use.		
	Classroom areas, materials, and supplies contain labels that include multiple communication forms that support the learners within the group (print, pictures, braille, tangible symbols, etc.).		
	Lighting is ample to accommodate visual needs, including reducing glare and ensuring optimal visibility.		
	Ambient and background noises (HVAC, hallway noise, other students, staff side conversations) are well-managed and do not distract students from the learning activity.		
	Classroom displays are minimized to essential information to support learning without excessive visual clutter.		
Materials and Instruction	Instructional materials are individualized for each learner across communication forms (print, pictures, braille, tangible symbols, etc.) and are in accessible formats (braille, large print, or digital).		
	Assistive technology (screen readers, magnifiers, slant boards, switches, etc.) is available, incorporated into the learning activity, fully functional, and familiar to students and staff.		
	A variety of high-quality literacy materials are available to students throughout the school day that relate to student interests, connect to the general education curriculum, and are contemporary and relevant.		

(Cont.)

TABLE 3.6 (Cont.)

	Yes	No
Individualized augmentative and alternative communication (AAC) supports and devices are available to students throughout the activity.		
The environment and instructional activities foster peer-to-peer interactions.		
Adults are responsive to student communication attempts, facilitate and sustain interactions, and encourage communicative behavior from all students.		

the multidisciplinary team and families to participate in this assessment process in order to obtain a clear understanding of the individual from a variety of perspectives and across different environments (Brady et al., 2016). Members of the multidisciplinary team include parents, special education and general education teachers, speech-language pathologists, physical and occupational therapists, and other related service personnel, such as TVIs and TODs. When each professional provides an accurate and meaningful understanding of the abilities the individual with extensive abilities possesses and goals for further development, a comprehensive program can be developed that truly supports the individual across areas of functioning. For example, a teacher of the visually impaired will be able to share the results of the most recent functional vision assessment, and the physical therapist can contribute information on the learner's motor abilities. Similarly, families can provide insight into the communication demands at home, as well as the learner's favorite activities, hobbies, and other areas of interest. Each category contains information on additional resources to consider to provide more information for a particular domain.

Assessment Resources

Table 3.2 provides a list of formal and informal tools that can support the assessment of communication and literacy skills.

Conclusion

Here are some points to consider when planning assessment for learners with extensive support needs:

- ♦ Before conducting any assessment with a learner who has extensive support needs, it is crucial to review the tool in advance. This ensures the learner has adequate access to the physical materials, can respond to the assessment directives, and helps determine if there is flexibility in presenting the items or in the ways the learner can showcase their skills.
- ♦ Consider pre-teaching or reviewing some of the tasks that the learner will experience during the assessment so that they are not experienced for the first time during the evaluation. For example, collaborating with a TVI before an FVA can ensure the learner understands how to respond to different items that will be presented during the assessment.
- ♦ Most assessments do not need to be completed in one session. Look to schedule lengthy assessments in segments so the learner is not fatigued.
- ♦ Ensure the assessor is familiar with the learner or directly supported by someone during the assessment session. This will help to ensure that an accurate understanding of the learner's skills is obtained and help to identify discrepancies in their skill demonstration or performance.

References

Adkins, A., Baltisberger, S., Kitchen, S., & Sewell, D. (2021). Early Tactile Learning Profile. Texas School for the Blind and Visually Impaired, Austin, TX.

Brady, N. C., Fleming, K., Romine, R. S., Holbrook, A., Muller, K., & Kasari, C. (2018a). Concurrent validity and reliability for the Communication Complexity Scale. *American Journal of Speech-Language Pathology*, 27(1), 237–246.

Brady, N. C., Matthews, K., Fleming, K., & Trujillo, H. (2018b). *CCS classroom: A direct observation tool for measuring communication in classrooms.* [unpublished manuscript]. University of Kansas.

Brady, N. C., Fleming, K., Thiemann-Bourque, K., Olswang, L., Dowden, P., Saunders, M. D., & Marquis, J. (2012). Development of the communication complexity scale. *American Journal of Speech-Language Pathology, 21*(1), 16–28.

Brady, N. C., Bruce, S., Goldman, A., Erickson, K., Mineo, B., Ogletree, B. T.,... & Wilkinson, K. (2016). Communication services and supports for individuals with severe disabilities: Guidance for assessment and intervention. *American Journal on Intellectual and Developmental Disabilities, 121*(2), 121–138.

Bruce, S. M. (2010). Holistic communication profiles for children who are deafblind. *AER Journal: Research and Practice in Visual Impairment and Blindness, 3*(3), 106–110.

Bruce, S. M., Ivy, S. E., & Brum, C. (2024). Severe and multiple disabilities. In J. M. Kauffman, D. P. Hallahan, & P. C. Pullen (Eds.), *Handbook of special education* (3rd ed., pp. 327–359). Routledge.

Bruce, S., Sacks, S., & Brum, C. (2016). Assessment of students who have visual impairments and additional disabilities. In S. Sacks & M. Zatta (Eds.), *Keys to educational success: Teaching students with visual impairments and multiple disabilities* (pp. 101–147). AFB Press.

Clendon, S., Paynter, J., Walker, S., Bowen, R., & Westerveld, M. F. (2021). Emergent literacy assessment in children with autism spectrum disorder who have limited verbal communication skills: A tutorial. *Language, Speech, and Hearing Services in Schools, 52*(1), 165–180. https://doi.org/10.1044/2020_LSHSS-20-00030

Goodman, K., & Hooks, L. (2016). Encouraging Family Involvement through Culturally Relevant Pedagogy. *SRATE Journal, 25*(2), 33–41.

Gunn, B., Simmons, D., & Kame'enui, E. (1995). Emergent literacy: Synthesis of the research (Technical Report No. 19). Retrieved October 30, 2024 from https://files.eric.ed.gov/fulltext/ED386866.pdf

Johns, J. L. (2005). *Basic reading inventory: Pre-primer through grade twelve and early literacy assessments.* Kendall Hunt. https://www.amazon.com/Basic-Reading-Inventory-Text-Only/dp/0006908292

Koenig, A. J., & Holbrook, M. C. (1995). *Learning media assessment of students with visual impairments: A resource guide for teachers.* Texas School for the Blind and Visually Impaired, Business Office, 1100 West 45th St., Austin, TX 78756-3494.

McIntyre, N. S., Loughran, C., & Towson, J. (2022). Reimagining assessment of literacy skills for adolescents with intellectual disabilities: A tutorial for an individualized approach. *Perspectives of the ASHA Special Interest Groups, 7*(6), 1606–1618.

Montgomery, C., & Graves, A. (2017). Information functional hearing evaluation (IFHE). Texas School for the Blind and Visually Impaired.

National Reading Panel (NRP). (2000). *A report of the national reading panel: Teaching children to read*. National Institute of Child Health and Human Development.

Nelson, C., & Bruce, S. (2019). Children who are deaf/hard of hearing with disabilities: Paths to language and literacy. *Education Sciences, 9*(134), 1–16.

Niemiec, R. M., & Tomasulo, D. (2023). Introduction to disability and strengths-based approaches. In D. Tomasulo & R. M. Niemiec (Eds.), *Character strengths and abilities within disabilities: Advances in science and practice* (pp. 3–22). Springer International Publishing.

Nowell, K. P., Bernardin, C. J., Brown, C., & Kanne, S. (2021). Characterization of special interests in autism spectrum disorder: A brief review and pilot study using the special interests survey. *Journal of Autism and Developmental Disorders, 51*(8), 2711–2724.

Rose, D. (2000). Universal design for learning. *Journal of Special Education Technology, 15*(4), 47–51.

Rowland, C. (2011). Using the communication matrix to assess expressive skills in early communicators. *Communication Disorders Quarterly, 32*(3), 190–201.

Ryndak., D. L., Orlando, A., & Burnette, K. K. (2020). Creating and implementing inclusive education. In F. Brown, J. McDonnell, & M. E. Snell (Eds.), *Instruction of students with severe disabilities* (9th ed., pp. 207–231). Pearson.

Watson, L., Boyd, B., Baranek, G., Crais, E., & Odom, S. (2011). Advancing Social Communication and Play (ASAP): An Intervention Program for Preschoolers with Autism. Unpublished manual, The University of North Carolina at Chapel Hill. Retrieved from: https://www.med.unc.edu/ahs/asap/wpcontent/uploads/sites/443/2017/09/ASAP-Book-I-Assessment-and-Intervention.pdf

Westling, D. L., Carter, E. W., Da Fonte, M. A., & Kurth, J. A. (2021). *Teaching students with severe disabilities* (6th ed.). Pearson.

Whitehurst, G. J., & Lonigan, C. J. (1998). Child development and emergent literacy. *Child Development, 69,* 848–872. https://doi.org/10.1111/j.1467-8624.1998.tb06247.x

4

Lesson Planning and Material Preparation

Preparing for a lesson is just as important as teaching it. Oftentimes, teachers have so many pieces to manage that it can be overwhelming and stressful thinking of all the components to include. When thinking about students with extensive support needs, there are even more things to consider, and it can be easy to forget or not take into account an aspect of your instruction that may be critical to a student's success with learning the content. Chapter 1 provided an overview of learners with extensive support needs, while Chapter 2 explored literacy considerations for this group of learners, and Chapter 3 focused on strategies and tools to assess communication and literacy skills. The information from these previous chapters will be essential for completing a lesson plan to guide the interactive reading lesson.

Comprehensive Lesson Planning

Appendix A provides a comprehensive lesson planning tool that highlights the abilities and areas that require additional support for learners with extensive support needs. Throughout this chapter, sections from the guide will be highlighted and described in detail. Chapters 2 and 3 provide useful assessment tools, strategies, and considerations to obtain relevant information to complete the guide. The tool can be adapted to meet the specific needs of a teacher, learner, or classroom and is intended to aid in the collection of information in multiple areas. It is recommended that teachers collaborate with other related service professionals familiar with the student with extensive support needs to collect information across disciplines. Depending on the services indicated in the individual's IEP, related service providers may include speech-language pathologist (SLP), occupational therapist (OT), physical therapist (PT), teacher of the blind and visually impaired (TVI), teacher of the deaf and hard of hearing (TOD), and certified orientation and mobility specialist (COMS). The following sections will provide guidance to completing the comprehensive lesson planning guide, while Chapters 5 and 6 will provide instructional strategies to utilize during the interactive reading lesson.

Part A: Learner Assets and Areas of Support

In the comprehensive lesson planning guide, it is important to include information relevant to the individual's assets and areas where they require support that may influence overall engagement in literacy. This information is important when determining the content (book selection and vocabulary), identifying the supports for access (physical and through all sensory channels), and integrating communication modes (across levels of complexity and through receptive and expressive channels). Table 4.1 describes Part A of the comprehensive lesson plan.

Background and Culture

Individuals with extensive support needs represent a group of learners with diverse abilities, experiences, and areas where they require support (Westling et al., 2021). An individual learner's diagnosis often will result in an interconnected and complex set of implications that, depending on the individual's age, can also include a rich history of services and supports (Giangreco et al., 2020). Families, especially parents, are the experts on their child with a disability, and it is vital to include the family perspective at this stage of planning. Aside from obtaining information on

TABLE 4.1 Part A: Learner Assets and Areas of Support

Personal Characteristics: Assess strengths and weaknesses in functioning, including areas of strength and necessary supports. Utilize the information covered and assessment resources from Chapters 2 and 3 to complete this section. Additionally, consultation with relevant related service personnel (SLP, OT, PT, TVI, TOD, COMS, etc.) is recommended.	
Background and Culture Aspects of the learner's history, background, and previous experiences that contribute to their identity	Diagnosis, medical history, and current health status: Culture: Family life and language at home: Interests:
Sensory Abilities Results from formal, informal, and functional assessments that demonstrate how information is received from each sensory channel	Vision: Hearing: Tactile: Learning media:
Motor Abilities Consider range of motion, strength, tone, and extent of voluntary control, as well as current equipment and positioning supports that are needed for optimal access to instruction and the learning environment	Fine motor: Gross motor: Adaptive equipment and positioning:
Communication Describe the complexity of the learner's communication modes, as well as supports they require (tangible symbols, speech-generating device, communication board, etc.)	Receptive communication modes: Expressive communication modes: Augmentative and Alternative communication (AAC):

the diagnosis, medical history, and current health status, families can also provide insight regarding the individual at home. Moreover, because communication challenges faced by individuals with extensive support needs often limit their ability for identity expression (Wofford et al., 2022), families can provide not only insight into home culture and language but also the likes, dislikes, preferences, and interests of the individual that would not be captured while at school.

Sensory Channels

Many individuals with extensive support needs experience some level of visual impairment and hearing loss support (Westling et al., 2021). Limited access to information through the primary information-gathering channels (vision and hearing) can create additional challenges when considering the interconnectedness of language and literacy (Allen & Morere, 2020). There is no one-size-fits-all set of strategies to support a student across all sensory channels, which highlights the importance of obtaining not only an accurate understanding of the learner's available vision and hearing but also a measure of their ability to access and utilize the residual vision and hearing they possess. Chapter 3 describes informal functional vision and hearing assessments that, when conducted in collaboration with the TVI, COMS, or TOD, can provide an effective means of determining the individual's abilities to exchange information via their primary sensory channels. Additionally, the Learning Media Assessment can help teams determine the best learning mode (visual, auditory, tactile, kinesthetic, or olfactory) for a student with a visual impairment (Koeing & Holbrook, 1995).

Motor Abilities

Understanding the amount of access to voluntary movement a learner with extensive support possesses is important when planning the individual's physical access to the learning activity. This includes moving their body to engage in interactions with materials and people (e.g., reaching for an item, grasping an object, or turning towards a peer who is speaking), accessing a speech-generating device (SGD), and navigating the learning environment. Physical access also includes overall body positioning so the individual can physically participate and have optimal access through their sensor channels, instructional adaptations, or material adaptations that may be needed to facilitate optimal access, and the use of specialized equipment to support positioning, access, and mobility throughout the activity. It is essential for classroom teachers and support staff to work with the physical therapist and occupational therapist to discuss physical access and to receive training on equipment use and care, as well as proper positioning and transferring techniques.

Communication
The ability to effectively interact with others is imperative to not only teaching and learning but also literacy instruction (Brady et al., 2016). Communication is multifaceted, with many factors influencing the exchange of information, including the messages being shared, the communication modes being used, the communication partner, and the environment where the interaction is occurring. Chapter 2 provides detailed information on strategies for communication development for learners with extensive support needs, while Chapter 3 provides assessment tools that can be used to determine the level of complexity of an individual's communication, as well as assessment considerations for learners with extensive support needs to support an accurate and useful understanding of their communication abilities can be obtained before instruction. Consultations with the SLP and family are important when assessing communication as well as when making decisions regarding specific communication modes to utilize with a learner.

Part B: Literacy Skills and Instructional Goals

Individuals with extensive support needs, just like their age-equivalent peers, will present with a range of literacy skills. However, the implications of their disability, especially related to communication and cognition, may have impacted their literacy skill development. Regardless of the individual's abilities, it is important to maintain high expectations. For learners with extensive support needs, including those with sensory impairments, literacy instruction starts with a comprehensive assessment of literacy skills (Bruce & Brum, 2025). Chapter 3 provides informal assessments to examine a learner's foundational reading abilities. It is important to note that some learners may require adaptations and modifications to the informal literacy assessment. For example, a student who communicates through gestures may be asked to point to a letter that makes a particular sound. Similarly, for a student who utilizes an SGD for expressive communication, a specific page on the device may need to be programmed before the assessment to ensure the individual has the means to express responses to each assessment item.

Regardless of a learner's abilities, they must be accessing the curriculum at their grade level. It is important to prioritize goals that strike a balance between the needs of the individual (determined through meaningful assessment) and meaningfully accessing grade-level state standards (Jimenez, 2020). Functional goals that directly connect to areas of skill development for the students can still be based on grade-level standards, with learning goals and objectives providing the entry points for the individual to access the content. Because of the interconnectedness of literacy and communication for learners with extensive support needs, the balance for literacy instruction includes goals that develop literacy skills, but all support engagement and communication development. Working with the SLP and other members of the multi-disciplinary team, including general education teachers, can serve as an effective means to identify literacy and communication goals that connect to state standards while also meeting the needs of the individual learner with extensive support needs. Table 4.2 describes Part B of the comprehensive lesson plan.

Part C: Lesson Preparation

There are steps involved in planning an effective interactive literacy lesson for individuals with extensive support needs. Part C of the Comprehensive Lesson Planning Guide will describe the process for text selection, adaptation, and modification, as needed for the specific individual or group of learners with extensive support needs (see Table 4.3). Each step will include examples and strategies to support planning efforts and ensure the needs of each individual are considered in the planning (and later implementation) of the activity.

TABLE 4.2 Part B: Literacy Skills and Instructional Goals

Literacy Skills Include information on the learner's skills and indicate, if necessary, accommodations or modifications that may be needed to support physical or communication abilities	Book handling: Conventions of print: Phoneme-grapheme correspondence: Phonemic awareness: Phonics: Fluency: Vocabulary: Comprehension:
Relevant Grade-level literacy standard(s)	
Instructional Goals When developing goals, consider the five cross-cutting themes: meaning making, language development, effective expression, content knowledge, and foundational skills	(1) (2) (3)

Step 1: Selecting a Text

Typically, we choose to read what we are interested in, so why wouldn't the same be true for our students? Including students and their interests in selecting the text is one way to support their motivation to participate in the lesson. Being intentional with text selection can also provide an opportunity to highlight a student's home culture and/or background that can support connections across home and school. After reviewing and aligning with grade-level content standards, the Sample Interest Inventory from Chapter 3 can serve as a great starting point to identify the learner's preferences, interests, and cultural and linguistic background to influence the selection of the text used during interactive reading.

TABLE 4.3 Part C: Lesson Preparation

Text Selection Consider student interests, home language and culture, grade-level books, current events, and experience books	Title of text:	
Text Modification Based on the student's physical abilities, level of communication complexity, and sensory abilities identify the types of modifications to the text that are necessary to ensure optimal access to the content. For each modification checked, used the column to the right to describe the specific changes in detail.	**Bypass Reading:** ❏ Change the modality ❏ Integrate AAC or technology **Decrease Reading:** ❏ Simplify vocabulary ❏ Change the storyline ❏ Decrease the amount of text ❏ Find an abridged version ❏ Simplify supplementary info **Support Reading:** ❏ Add repeated story line ❏ Add supplementary representations ❏ Objects ❏ Images ❏ Textures ❏ Other ❏ Enhance with textures ❏ Increase durability ❏ Add page turners **Guide & Organize Reading:** ❏ Graphic organizers ❏ Integrate multiple communication modes ❏ Structured notes	Modification details:
Learning Environment Ensure the learning environmental is intentionally arranged to support the learner's access and participation	Seating/positioning arrangements for the student: Classroom staff support during the activity: Ambient concerns:	

Here are some strategies to consider when selecting a text:

♦ *What broad categories is the student interested in?* Think about vehicles, music, animals, dinosaurs, etc. Broader categories are a good place to start when searching for a commercially produced text. Remember, the age appropriateness of a book is important.
♦ *Think about the student's home culture and primary language.* Are there events or traditions that you can focus on at certain times of the year? Think about holidays, festivals, and celebrations. Can you find a book of interest to the student where key vocabulary can also be translated into their home language?
♦ *What books, genres, or other materials are being read by the student's grade-level peers?* Connect with general-education teachers to see what they are currently reading or will be reading in the upcoming months. Starting a book before it is read by general-education peers is a great strategy to support the involvement of the learner with extensive support needs in inclusion and class discussions. Learning about the book before entering the inclusive classroom will allow the learner to become familiar with the content and vocabulary and have experience accessing the information on their communication board or device.
♦ *Consider focusing on current events.* Websites from trusted and vetted sources allow you to adjust Lexile levels to create broader access for students with varying reading abilities without sacrificing content. For example, TweenTribune.com is produced by the Smithsonian Museum and has a variety of high-interest articles for all ages that even include some pictures. See Table 4.4 for a list of online and curricular resources.
♦ *Get the students involved.* After curating some options that you think will appeal to your students, let them pick what you will read! Including your students in the selection of the text can be a great way to start engaging them in the lesson from the beginning. Selecting three current events topics or three books about different vehicles can

TABLE 4.4 Resources for Selecting Text for Interactive Reading

Online Resources

Monarch Reader	Free open-source library with over 77,000 books.	https://monarchreader.com/
Tween Tribune	Current events articles with adjustable Lexile levels and images.	www.tweentribune.com
Newsela	High-interest articles that provide student performance feedback to teachers.	www.newsela.com
Achieve 3000	Web-based platform offering nonfiction texts differentiated by Lexile level.	www.achieve3000.com
Read180	Integrated program for reading comprehension, writing, and vocabulary.	www.hmhco.com/products/read-180/family/
Curricular Resources		
Building with Stories	Early literacy skills curriculum with adapted commercially produced texts and supplementary objects.	https://www.attainmentcompany.com/building-stories
Teaching to the Standards: English Language Arts	Adapted secondary grade-level texts with graphic supports that are aligned with the common core curriculum.	www.attainmentcompany.com/teaching-standardsenglish-language-arts

allow you to make connections with grade-level standards while also including students in the process and targeting their interests.

- *Stick to general criteria.* When first implementing interactive reading, try finding a book that is about 10–15 pages, with a similar number of words on each page, and with images related to the story content that support comprehension of the written text. Additionally, look for a text with clear key vocabulary repeated throughout the story or with consistent characters.

It may be difficult to find a commercially produced book that meets every student's needs. Even commercially produced

> *Quickly create your own e-books.* For students who require physical support, e-books are a great way to support literacy engagement. Use a tablet to take pictures of each page of the physical book. Next, use the pictures to create a slide deck with one picture per slide. Then, narrate the slide deck so that the story can be read to the individual. You can also integrate comprehension questions throughout the story. Now, using a tablet, computer, or large display, present the slide deck for the individual to view and hear. For further engagement, allow the learner to advance the slides to "turn the page" using the touchscreen, mouse, or adapted Bluetooth switch.

adapted curricula targeted to students with extensive support needs will most likely need further modification or adaptation. Remember, students, regardless of age, love to hear and see themselves integrated into the curriculum. Creating a unique book can be as easy as taking pictures during an engaging activity and writing a simple narrative to accompany it. The pictures and text can be put together into a slide deck for digital access or printed into a physical book. Table 4.4 contains a list of resources for finding a text to use for interactive reading with learners with extensive support needs.

Strategy Focus: Creating Experience Books

Experience books are a personalized and individualized literacy activity that allows a child to share a lived experience without needing to rely on text. Often used for learners who are deafblind, experience books are relevant to all learners who require support to access traditional literacy materials. It is a way to trigger memories about a meaningful experience and create communication opportunities for the child to express themselves while creating and reading the book. When starting to develop an experience book, remember that the child is involved in the writing of the book.
  Here are the steps involved in creating an experience book:

1. *Collect artifacts during the experience.* Consider saliency or what is most important to the child throughout the experience. Objects should be used, preferably those used during the experience, like candles from a birthday cake. Photographs are also a great way to capture highlights from the experience.
2. *Involve the student in the development of the book.* Consider the format of the book and ensure the learner can access it as independently as possible in a format that they can hold and with pages they can turn. Add an object to each page of the book using Velcro so that they can be easily removed and actions can be recreated. For example, a whisk can be added to a page to represent mixing the cake batter.

3. *Think about vocabulary.* What were significant names or actions that were central to the experience? Add a written description to each page that captures the different parts of the experience, highlighting key vocabulary throughout. Add supplementary supports, such as braille labels to keywords, textures, etc., to support engagement and understanding.
4. *Keep it accessible.* Have a designated area for the experience book so that the child can access the book throughout the day. This will allow the child to spontaneously indicate that they want to read the book by pointing to it or bringing it to you.

Step 2: Modifying the Text

Text adaptations or modifications for a learner with extensive support needs are based on identified areas of support. Adaptations may be necessary when the learner has trouble with decoding, comprehension, or access through vision, hearing, or physically handling the material (Lane & Ruppar, 2018). Changing a text to better suit the learner's needs can be done with the content or the physical book. This includes adding supports to increase understanding, limiting the information presented, or increasing the physical accessibility of the book.

It may be necessary to change the book to increase the student's understanding of the content or storyline. When thinking about changing the content of a book, a question to keep asking is: how can this book change to increase the student's comprehension of the content? The changes made might be specific to an individual learner, so keep in mind that you may need different versions of a book for a small group or whole class to have meaningful access. Common adaptations for learners with extensive support needs involve modifying or supplementing the text (Dyke & Pemberton, 2002). These include:

Bypass reading to increase engagement and listening comprehension. Here, the focus is on the student understanding the text instead of reading and understanding.

- *Change the modality* by having the text read aloud to a partner.
- *Integrate technology* by integrating the text into a slide deck that is narrated or utilizing AAC, such as an SGD (tablet

or single/multiple level switch) to read the entire text or page by page.

Decrease reading by reducing the amount and/or complexity of the text. This can support learners who are able to decode text but at a slower rate or reduced level of complexity. Strategies to decrease reading include:

- *Simplify the vocabulary.* Some technical or industry terms may not be at a level that is accessible to the students. If that is the case, consider using different terms for key vocabulary. Also, consider incorporating key terms from other books to create connections across books.
- *Change the storyline* by omitting portions of the text. There are often subplots in a text that contribute to the overall plot. This is especially true in chapter books. Consider limiting and removing subplots or changing the main plot of the text to reduce its complexity. To maintain interest, details can be slowly added during repeated readings.
- *Decrease the amount of text.* If there is too much text on a page, remove details that do not impact the overall plot. This can be easily done by using a highlighter to enhance the lines of text to be read in the adapted version. If you would like to also visually decrease the amount of text on the page, use packing tape to secure a new section of text over the existing material. This also allows elements to be added to support students with visual impairments (contrast, large print, bold typeface).
- *Create or find an abridged version.* For chapter books, finding a version that is already shortened can be very helpful.
- *Reduce and simplify supplementary information.* For some learners, additional information, such as pictures or detailed page layouts, can distract from the content.

Support reading by adding features to increase comprehension and engagement of the material. This includes incorporating supplementary materials to aid understanding and can serve as an opportunity to incorporate additional communication modes.

- *Add a repeated storyline.* Changing the text can also mean adding information to support understanding, such as a repeated storyline that represents the main plot of the book or section. When developing the sentence to use, remember to consider key vocabulary and provide vehicles for students to repeat the storyline (e.g., programming an AAC device).
- *Add supplementary representations.* Intentionally select objects or pictures can be added to the text to represent key vocabulary or concepts that are integral to the text. These supplementary representations can also serve as an alternate means for a learner to respond and participate in the interactive reading.
- *Enhance the text with textures.* Textures are a great multisensory addition to text that can increase understanding and interest. In addition to serving as a support for students with visual impairments in interacting with the text, examples include adding sand to a rough surface or feathers to a bird. Braille labels can also be added to add a sensory component and highlight important words or phrases.
- *Increase durability.* It may be necessary to modify the physical book so that a student can appropriately handle and interact with the text. This may even include changing the format of the book. To increase durability, remove the book's binding, laminate the pages, and then add a spiral binding or a three-hole binder, which can make the text sturdier. Just be cautious, as lamination adds glare to the pages and may not suit students with visual impairments.
- *Add page-turners.* Felt circles, construction paper, or popsicle sticks can build up page corners to make them easier to turn.

Guide and organize reading by incorporating graphic organizers to support text access and comprehension.

- **Graphic organizers** that are familiar to the student can help to organize content and support participation in a discussion or provide a structure for writing a summary.

- *Integrating multiple communication modes* into the graphic organizer, such as pictures, can reduce the cognitive demand of the activity and support communication during the activity.
- *Structured notes* can help students identify important information that can result in a summary or study guide. The teacher creates a form for the student to add information while the text is read. For example, definitions can be listed in a structured notes document where the student would add the vocabulary word when it is encountered in the text. This would result in a list of vocabulary words and definitions but reduce the cognitive demand for the student by not requiring them to write out each definition.

It is important to remember that content changes to a book do not need to be permanent or for every version of the book being read at one time. Removed and changed aspects can be reintroduced during repeated readings to build complexity and maintain interest. Also, multiple copies of the same text with different types of modifications can create a classroom set of books to support various learning needs throughout the years.

Text modifications to increase access for a learner with extensive support needs can be permanent or temporary. Using the text *Ed Roberts: Champion of Disability Rights,* written by Diana Pastora Carson, rough adhesive glitter tape can be added to the cover to add texture to highlight the title and author (see Figure 4.1). Depending on the learner's tactile skills raised puff paint or a hot glue gun could be used to trace the letters of the title, while a clear braille label could also be included as an additional representation.

For a temporary modification to the text to reduce the visual information on the cover, an overlay made of construction paper can be added to the cover (see Figure 4.2). This is a quick and temporary modification to the book that can easily be removed for a learner who does not require reduced visual information.

Text modifications can also include using the original material to influence the development of a simpler version of the text. For example, Figure 4.3 is an example of pages from the text without

FIGURE 4.1 Example of book cover with added textures around the title and under the author's name

FIGURE 4.2 Example of a simplified book cover with temporary overlay

Lesson Planning and Material Preparation ◆ 77

FIGURE 4.3 Original pages from picture book

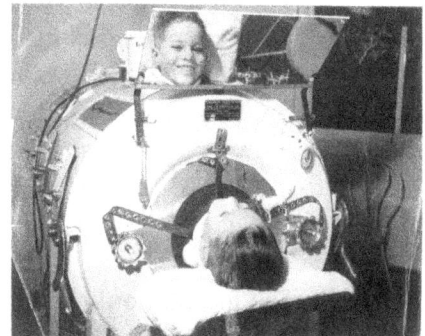

FIGURE 4.4 Modified pages from a book with a photograph added and simplified text

any changes. The picture is somewhat abstract and potentially difficult for a learner with extensive support needs to discern. Additionally, the text includes a significant amount of information that may not be necessary for a learner to glean the key facts from the text.

Using the original text, Figure 4.4 demonstrates how a modified version can be developed that maintains the essence of the original book. The simplified image or the modified text could be adhered to the physical book, or a new version of the book could be created by printing the new pages or digitally by embedding the image and text into a slide deck that could be easily narrated and a switch used to advance each page.

Step 3: Arranging the Environment

The arrangement of a learning environment can influence the success of any instructional activity. Think about creating flexible spaces that can change to suit your student's needs and maximize their physical access to the activity. Some materials can be student-accessible for students to interact with outside of structure lessons. Think about it: It is nearly impossible to learn how to handle a book without ever having the opportunity to physically hold one.

Here are some ways you can arrange the environment to support engagement:

- *Make some materials accessible to students.* Designate an area in the classroom where books are physically accessible to your students. Granting them continuous access can open up opportunities for communication. At some point during the school day, a student may bring you their favorite book, "asking" you to read with them. Without access, there are fewer opportunities for them to initiate the interaction.
- *Be flexible with positioning.* Ideally, the adult should be at eye level with their students. However, for some students, a reclined position may provide better access to the lesson material. For example, a student who struggles with neck control may have better access (and require fewer prompts to keep their head up) in a reclined position in their wheelchair or on a beanbag chair on the floor. Similarly, a student who requires trunk support may access the lesson more effectively in a prone stander with a tray.
- *Consider vision and hearing.* When determining where a student will sit during the lesson, consider the student's field of vision and hearing loss. Depending on their type

of visual impairment, the student may need to be seated in close proximity, to the side, or have their own enlarged copy of the text presented on a slant board. Students with lateral hearing loss will need to sit directly in front of you or with their less-impacted ear in your direction.
- *Pay attention to the ambiance.* Try your best to keep the immediate setting clearly defined, distraction-free, and conducive to the child's needs. Ambient noise, glare, and lighting shift and change throughout the day and may affect a student with sensory sensitivities.

Interactive reading can be implemented with the adult and child seated at a table or on the floor as long the arrangement works with the student's needs. If the learner needs space to move their body, the floor may be better suited for implementation, rather than at a table where the child must be cued to remain in their seat. The environment should be structured in a way that elicits and supports interactions with the text and any supplementary items.

Step 4: Planning for Data Collection

Measuring progress is vital and the only means of assessing what has been learned from a learning activity. Data collection begins in the planning phase and should be thought about well before the lesson begins. This starts with establishing clear student learning outcomes that measure what the student is expected to have accomplished at the end of the lesson. This also includes clear achievement criteria and setting up methods to collect information throughout the learning activity. Remember, the learning outcomes may be individualized among your students – meaning, they may all be working on different skills during the same activity.

Conclusion

Here are some considerations when planning for interactive reading:

- Use your assessments as a starting point. Develop student learning outcomes from the information you collected in your assessments (see Chapter 3). Create a plan of what you expect each student to accomplish. The plan can be revised over time, but having a sense of where you want to go is important.
- Focus on key vocabulary and story comprehension. Once you have selected a text, begin to identify key vocabulary and important aspects of the material that you intend for your students to learn. Chapter 5 will help you to integrate vocabulary and comprehension probes during your reading.
- Intentionally collect data the data you need. Create data sheets that are easy to use, only measure the targeted student learning outcome, and provide you with visual information over time. Focus on the target skill, especially the level of accuracy and support provided. Also, arranging your data sheets to provide visual information saves you time in the future. See Appendix B for a data sheet to be used with interactive reading.
- Use your classroom staff to help with data collection, individual student support, or material management during the lesson. Arrange responsibilities and adult seating/positioning before the lesson begins so that everyone understands their responsibilities and intended location from the start.
- Do your best to decrease the moving parts of the lesson. Have materials prepared and organized for each student in advance. Often, bins can be an easy way to have all of the materials in one place. Wasting time looking for something when you have your students in front of you and ready to learn will lead to distraction.

References

Allen, T. E., & Morere, D. A. (2020). Early visual language skills affect the trajectory of literacy gains over a three-year period of time for preschool aged deaf children experience signing in the home. *PLoS ONE, 15*(2), e0229591.

Brady, N. C., Bruce, S., Goldman, A., Erickson, K., Mineo, B., Ogletree, B. T.,... & Wilkinson, K. (2016). Communication services and supports for individuals with severe disabilities: Guidance for assessment and intervention. *American Journal on Intellectual and Developmental Disabilities, 121*(2), 121–138.

Bruce, S., & Brum, C. (2025). Emergent literacy in individuals who are deafblind. In T. Hartshorne, M. J. Janssen, & W. Wittich (Eds.), *Volume II: Learning, education and support of deafblind children and adults: An interdisciplinary approach. Series: Perspectives in deafness*. Oxford University Press.

Dyck, N., & Pemberton, J. B. (2002). A model for making decisions about text adaptations. *Intervention in School and Clinic, 38*(1), 28–35.

Giangreco, M. F., Shogren, K. A., & Dymond, S. K. (2020). Educating students with severe disabilities: Foundational concepts and practices. In F. Brown, J. McDonnell, & M. E. Snell (Eds.), *Instruction of students with severe disabilities: Meeting the needs of children and youth with intellectual disabilities, multiple disabilities, and autism spectrum disorders* (9th ed., pp. 1–27). Pearson.

Jimenez, B. (2020). Using assessment for planning standards-based individualized education programs. In D. M. Browder, F. Spooner, & G. R. Courtade (Eds.), *Teaching students with moderate and severe disabilities* (2nd ed., pp. 143–159). Guilford Press.

Koenig, A. J., & Holbrook, M. C. (1995). *Learning media assessment of students with visual impairments: A resource guide for teachers*. Texas School for the Blind and Visually Impaired, Business Office, 1100 West 45th St., Austin, TX 78756-3494.

Lane, L., & Ruppar, A. L. (2018). Adapting books and other literacy genres. In S. R. Copeland & E. B. Keefe (Eds.), *Effective literacy instruction for learners with complex needs* (2nd ed., pp. 273–296). Paul H. Brookes Publishing Co.

Westling, D. L., Carter, E. W., Da Fonte, M. A., & Kurth, J. A. (2021). *Teaching students with severe disabilities*. Pearson.

Wofford, M. C., Ogletree, B. T., & De Nardo, T. (2022). Identity-focused practice in augmentative and alternative communication services: A framework to support the intersecting identities of individuals with severe disabilities. *American Journal of Speech-Language Pathology, 31*(5), 1933–1948.

5

Implementing Interactive Reading

Effective literacy instruction for learners with extensive support needs is comprehensive and develops multiple literacy skills simultaneously through daily, interactive, and engaging daily activities that focus on constructing meaning (Erickson, 2017). Interactive reading (also known as shared or dialogic reading) is a literacy intervention where a text is read aloud, and interactions about the text are supported before, during, and after reading have proven to improve literacy and communication outcomes for learners with extensive support needs, including emergent literacy, vocabulary, and comprehension skills (Toews et al., 2021). Interactive reading allows a learner with extensive support needs to continue acquiring literacy skills while gleaning the benefits from literacy before they have the ability to independently decode text and extract meaning. Several instructional strategies have led to positive outcomes for developing listening comprehension skills with students with extensive support needs, including least-to-most prompting, time delay, instruction on wh-words, text comprehension strategies, and integrating technology (Dessemontet et al., 2024). This chapter will cover the implementation of interactive reading for learners with extensive support needs, including developing vocabulary, emergent literacy, and comprehension.

Systematic Instruction

The principle of systematic instruction is derived from applied behavior analysis and describes learning as a behavior change process, which can also include the establishment of new behaviors (Alberto & Troutman, 2021). For students with extensive support needs, systematic instruction is considered the most effective for teaching the standards across all content areas and appropriate when supporting students individually, in small groups, or in general education (Westling et al., 2021).

Following an antecedent-behavior-consequence (ABC) structure, the sequence of systematic instruction includes first securing the learner's attention, providing prompts to elicit the desired behavior, and determining the number of trials or attempts the learner will have to demonstrate the behavior (Collins, 2022).

Securing the Learner's Attention

Before instruction can fully begin, it is important to be sure you have the learner's attention. To ensure the learner is attending and ready, a *general attentional cue*, like a simple question such as, "Are you ready to work?" or a directive such as, "Look at me," provides an opportunity for the learner to respond to the question or directive in a variety of ways to indicate they are ready. For example, they could verbally indicate they are ready through voice or a speech-generating device (SGD), look at the teacher, or sit quietly while waiting for the activity to begin. For some students with extensive support needs who may be easily distracted or with sensory impairments, a more direct approach using a *specific attentional cue* may be required to secure the learner's attention where the learner is expected to demonstrate a specific action. For example, directing a student to show they are "ready to learn" and expecting them to respond by sitting with their hands clasped on the table or asking a student, "Can you touch your ears so I know you are listening?" and expecting them to stop talking, touch their ears, and look at the speaker. Other examples of specific attentional cues include asking a student to point to a word before reading it or to look at both options of flashcards before making a selection.

Prompts

Prompts are a type of scaffolding that can be provided to a learner to support their demonstration of a correct response. They can occur prior to instruction to increase the chances the learner will demonstrate the correct response or as response prompts that are integrated into the instructional sequence following a prompt hierarchy (Figure 5.1) to ensure error-less learning (an error rate of 20% or less during an instructional session). It is important to consider learner characteristics before providing prompts. For example, auditory prompts can be helpful if the student has a thorough understanding of the directional terms being utilized (i.e., "move it up" or "turn it to the left"). Similarly, learners with limited vision may have trouble accessing visual prompts that include rapid movements or are provided outside of their visual field. Additionally, it is also important to remember not to be overly direct with prompts to maintain joint attention with the learner through equal and active engagement in the activity (Kasari et al., 2022).

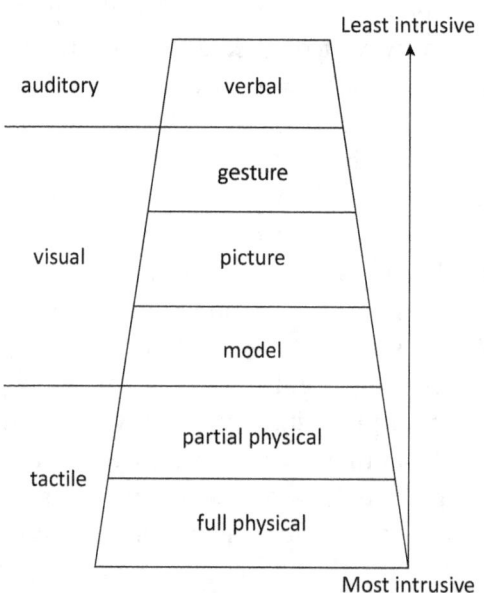

FIGURE 5.1 Prompt hierarchy

System of Least-to-Most Prompts

Table 5.1 provides an expanded hierarchy with descriptions of the different levels of prompts, as well as examples to support implementation at each level.

There are specific considerations to keep in mind when utilizing a prompt hierarchy:

- Always begin with the least-intrusive prompt. However, once familiar with the learner and their abilities, it may be appropriate to be at a more intrusive prompt level.
- Provide a specific prompt only once, and do not repeat prompts during a given trial. If the learner does not respond, progress to a higher level of prompt until the target skill is demonstrated.
- Once the learner has demonstrated the target skill, prompts begin to fade to increase independence.
- Before planning out a prompt hierarchy, be sure to consider the learner's physical and sensory abilities, as well as their understanding of positional terms, to ensure they can fully benefit from each level of prompting that is being provided.
- Provide ample time for the learner to comprehend the prompt that was provided and for them to provide a response. The amount of time will vary across individuals.
- Ensure the learner's attention has been secured before providing a prompt.

Time Delay

Time delay, casually known as wait time, is a highly effective procedure for teaching academic content to students with extensive support needs (Brown et al., 2019). After securing the learner's attention, a specific amount of lag time must be identified between when a request or direction is provided and when a prompt is delivered. The specific time delay can increase over time or remain constant and is measured in seconds, often starting with a 0-second delay to ensure error-less learning. Based on the specific learner's abilities and support needs, a longer

TABLE 5.1 Expanded Prompt Hierarchy

	Sensory Channel	Level of Assistance	Description	Implementation Example
Least Intrusive ↑↓		Independent	The learner correctly responds without support	
	Auditory	General Verbal Prompt	Ask the learner an open-ended question or provide a general comment	"What comes next" "What do you have?"
		Specific Verbal Prompt	Provide the learner with a verbal model or directions	"You can say, 'animal'" "Point to the picture"
	Visual	Gestural Prompt	Use a simple action to support the learner to achieve the response	Pointing to the correct object from a field of three items
		Photographic Prompt	Provide a photograph or visual model or example	A visual task analysis with the steps for hand washing
		Model Prompt	Demonstrate the desired behavior to the learner	Mimic lathering soap during hand washing
	Tactile	Partial Physical Prompt	A gentle touch for attention or to indicate movement	Tap the learner's elbow to cue reaching
Most Intrusive		Full Physical Prompt	Hand-under-hand or hand-over-hand guidance to perform an action	Placing a hand over the learner's hand for support to write their name

amount of time may be necessary. For example, if provided an array of items or pictures to choose from, a learner may require time to review all of the options before they can make a selection. Similarly, if they are expected to make a response using an SGD, time must be built in to reach the device, find the correct page and/or cell on the display, and select the correct cell to produce the response. A single least-intrusive prompt is provided after the delay that is most likely to support the learner in demonstrating the target skill and can be delivered across all instructional trials. It is unique to the individual learner and, as mentioned above, must be accessible to the learner given their physical and sensory abilities. After the prompt is provided, an additional delay is imposed to allow the learner to respond. If the response is correct, the learner is praised, and, if incorrect, an additional prompt is provided. Figure 5.2 provides a helpful visual of the

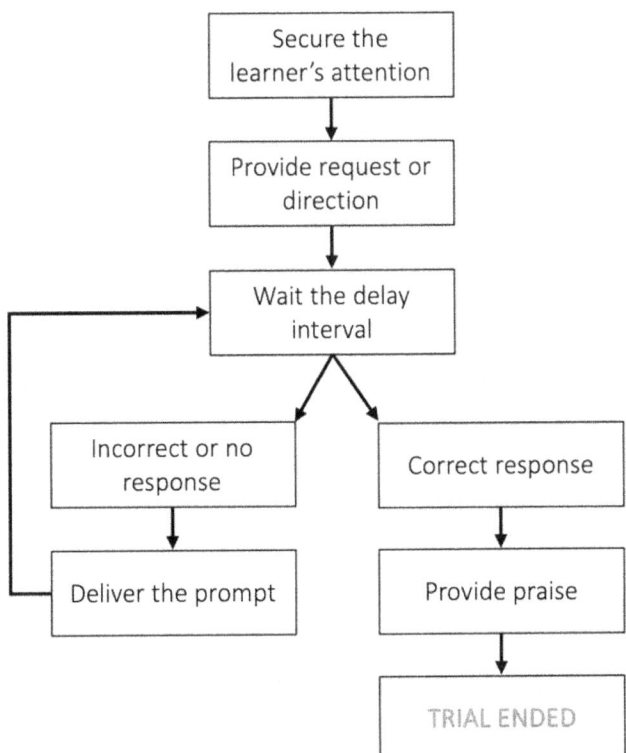

FIGURE 5.2 Time-delay process

time-delay process. It is important to note that the delay interval may need to be reduced for subsequent opportunities to limit the number of errors and reduce opportunities for guessing.

Instructional Trials

The antecedent-behavior-consequence (ABC) structure is what composes an instructional trial. Depending on the target skill, a learning session can include a single or multiple trials or attempts to demonstrate the target skill. The frequency of instructional trials ranges from multiple trials in rapid succession (e.g., spelling vocabulary words) to single trials that are embedded throughout a school day (e.g., responding to a greeting).

Vocabulary Development

The National Reading Panel (2000) explains that rich and explicit vocabulary instruction is a critical area of literacy and communication development for all individuals and details guidelines for vocabulary instruction. This includes active, direct, and systematic instruction, repetition, frequent exposure, consistent use in multiple environments, and integration of technology. For students with extensive support needs, this most likely will require the use of augmentative and alternative communication (AAC). The process of teaching new vocabulary words using AAC begins with providing clear descriptions of the words and how they are used and then maximizing opportunities to encounter and interact with the words through a range of instructional activities (Geist & Erickson, 2022). These include providing examples and non-examples, word associations, generating examples, word relationships, sentence generation, and identifying how the vocabulary is used in the context of a story.

Selecting Vocabulary for Instruction

When determining specific vocabulary to teach, the goal is to build on the learner's current vocabulary. It is essential to select high-utility words that the learner will encounter in multiple contexts across academic activities and that are not already known and understood (Erickson & Koppenhaver, 2020). For all learners, including those with extensive support needs, there are basic principles for selecting vocabulary words to teach focus on the three tiers of words (Beck et al., 2013):

- **Tier 1** includes basic and common words that are highly familiar to most individuals and that often appear in informal language interactions (e.g., cold, boy, house, play). Individuals will typically learn these words on their own. Additionally, the core vocabulary used in AAC system development typically includes mostly this group of words.
- **Tier 2** is made up of high-utility and wide-ranging words that are more academically focused and less often heard in everyday conversations (e.g., analyze, explain, measure, determine). These words are usually intentionally taught but can be used across content areas. For example, one can analyze an author's perspective in English class and analyze economic trends in math. Understanding words from this tier is an essential part of successful reading comprehension.
- **Tier 3** words are rare and technical words that are nuanced and often do not have utility outside of their immediate context or domain (e.g., electrolyte, circumference, osmosis, inflation). These words are typically learned for a specific purpose.

For students with extensive support needs, if the learner has acquired a significant number of Tier 1 words, it is important to focus instruction on acquiring high-utility Tier 2 words that can be used across multiple domains (Erickson & Koppenhaver, 2020). For example, when selecting vocabulary to teach from a fairy tale, a Tier 3 word such as "castle" and "princess" have much less utility compared to Tier 2 words like "challenge" and "overcome," which can be used in other situations that do not involve the story. Additionally, for students using AAC, the expressive vocabulary they can typically access is limited to the available words or phrases within their communication system. Consider selecting new words for the student to learn that can be defined using the existing vocabulary the student has available within their AAC system.

When selecting words to teach, remember that Tier 2 high-utility words are the most likely to be generalized beyond the interaction with the text; however, these terms may be more abstract. It is important to consult with multidisciplinary team members, especially the speech-language pathologist (SLP) and other relevant related service personnel, before selecting vocabulary. After the specific terms have been selected, it is important to identify the communication modes the learner will be utilizing for their expressive and receptive vocabulary (for more information on identification and assessment of communication modes, see Chapters 2 and 3). Options for expressive vocabulary can also change modes from lesson to lesson. Consider how the vocabulary will be presented to the student (receptive input) and also how they will express each word (expressive output), understanding that the communication form identified for input and output may not be the same. For example, a teacher may present three cards with a picture and text label that depict vocabulary from the story and ask the student to use their voice or a pointing gesture to indicate their response.

Introducing Vocabulary

It is critical to introduce the learner to the vocabulary before testing their abilities to identify the key terms. Vocabulary instruction can begin by allowing the learner to explore each representation while the word is provided to reduce the novelty. This is especially important for learners with visual impairments and who are deafblind so that they can utilize other sensory channels (touch, smell, hearing, etc.) to become familiar with each representation. Introducing the learner to the vocabulary can also involve the learner's SGD but supporting them to navigate to the correct page and, together, striking the button or cell to generate the word allows the individual to not only locate the cell or button but also begin to pair it with the verbal output from the device. Introducing vocabulary can take place at the start of each lesson and gradually fade as the student begins to make progress with identifying each representation.

Building Scaffolding Through Constant Time Delay

Before starting the interactive reading, it is important to teach key vocabulary and definitions using constant time delay (Hudson, 2020). Time delay is an effective procedure for teaching vocabulary to students with extensive support needs (Browder et al., 2009; Orlando & Ruppar, 2016). As mentioned above, the procedure allows for a consistent time period to elapse between a cue and the reinforcement for a child to produce the desired. Using representations for vocabulary and the learner's SGD, teaching key terms from the story and their definitions can start with a 0-second delay where the correct response is immediately presented to the student. For example, this can consist of displaying three vocabulary representations (cards, objects, pictures) and asking the student to "show me [word]" and immediately pointing to the correct representation, with the same structure also utilized for teaching definitions.

Steps for Teaching Vocabulary

Before vocabulary instruction begins, key terms must be identified. It is recommended that in consultation with the SLP and other related service personnel, Tier 2 words are selected to encourage generalization across content areas.

1. Secure the learner's attention.
2. Introduce each term by pairing it with the representation and allowing the learner time to explore each one.
3. Provide a directive to indicate the vocabulary word, for example, "Show me the [term]."
4. Implement the delay between the directive and the correct answer, starting with a 0-second delay.
   a. If the student indicates the correct term, provide positive praise, record the data, and continue to the next term.
   b. If the student is incorrect, non-responsive, or a 0-second delay is being implemented, then provide the correct response. This may include simply saying the term, activating the learner's SGD, or pairing forms, like stating the term and simultaneously pointing to the representation.

Note: If the delay has increased above zero and the learner provides three incorrect responses in a row, return to a 0-second delay for the remainder of the session.

5. Collect data on the accuracy of the learner's response, prompts required, and the interval of the time delay between the directive and answer.
6. Repeat for each term.

Developing Emergent Literacy Skills

After vocabulary instruction, it is time to shift focus to the development of emerging literacy skills, specifically book handling and print concepts. Here is where the learner will begin to engage with the physical text. It is essential to review the Foundational Literacy Skills and Literacy Environment assessments provided in Chapter 3 to gain an understanding of the learner's current skills related to literacy and where instruction should begin.

Target emergent literacy skills can be modeled throughout the interactive reading session and supported through a prompt sequence adapted from dialogic reading known as the PERM sequence (Whitehurst et al., 1988). The PERM mnemonic serves as a memory aid for the teacher to encourage the learner to demonstrate the target skills throughout the activity and provide support when needed.

It includes:

- **P**rompt the learner to express the target skill,
- **E**valuate their response and prompt (if necessary),
- **R**einforce a successful attempt or,
- **M**odel the skill (if the attempt was incorrect).

The PERM sequence can also be supported by the principles of systematic instruction, including utilizing a system of least-intrusive prompts (Figure 5.1) and constant time delay (Figure 5.2). To integrate these components, after the initial prompt in the PERM sequence, a time delay is imposed (i.e., 5–10 seconds) to allow time for the learner to respond. If the learner is incorrect or does not respond, the adult begins with a least-intrusive auditory (i.e., "turn the page") or visual prompt, such as a gesture (i.e., pointing to the right edge of the page) or modeling the desired behavior (i.e., lifting the edge the page) and wait for the student to respond. This sequence is repeated throughout the book reading to provide multiple opportunities for demonstration of the target emergent literacy skills.

Supporting Reading Comprehension

Systematic reading instruction can support the development of listening and reading comprehension for students with extensive support needs when they are actively engaged in the process of extracting meaning from text (Copeland et al., 2018). When taught using explicit instruction (modeling, guided and independent practice, and corrective feedback), learners acquired strategies for effective reading comprehension, including predicting, summarizing, paraphrasing, and identifying main ideas (Joseph et al., 2023).

Gaining the Learner's Attention

Securing and maintaining learner attention, as well as promoting active engagement throughout interactive reading, is critical. This can be accomplished by adding a "secure attention" prompt before instruction to gain attention and supporting interactions during reading to sustain attention throughout the activity (Whalon et al., 2015). After turning a page, the adult can draw attention to an aspect of the text to establish joint attention with the learner. This can be accomplished by a verbal prompt (e.g., "Look at this!") or a nonverbal gesture, such as pointing. Additional strategies can also be considered, such as a flashlight to visually highlight an aspect of the page or pointing between a picture in the text and a supplementary object that was included for the intervention.

Activating Prior Knowledge

Identifying texts that relate to the learner's interests and prior experiences with academic content is a way to support and sustain meaningful engagement with the content. Before reading, it is important to set the context for the text and see what the student knows about the topic. One strategy is talking with the student (and their family) about their experiences with the topic that can be shared with the group. A part of this activity can include having students identify vocabulary that relates to the topic or that is relevant to their experience. For students unfamiliar with the topic, a short video can provide not only background knowledge but also gain learner interest in the subject.

Here is an example of how to activate prior knowledge:

- Before reading a non-fiction text about the history of piñatas, a teacher can communicate with each student and their family to see if they have ever attended a party that had a piñata, including their own birthday party. For some students, this may be a typical part of their home culture, while others may be familiar with the concept, possibly by attending an event that included a piñata, whereas others may not have ever had an experience with one.
- Before beginning the conversation with students, the teacher can introduce the concept by showing a short video for students with experience with the event to begin making connections and to serve as an introduction and tangible example for those without any familiarity with the event or concept.
- For the students who have some experience with piñatas, they can then share their experiences verbally, using a pre-recorded message from a family member or by sharing photographs from the experience to make connections and provide examples to other students.
- During this exchange, the group can then begin to develop a list of relevant vocabulary that can support comprehension of the text that is about to be read.

Reading Intentions
Before reading or listening to a text, reading comprehension outcomes can be improved when students with extensive support needs have a clear purpose or reason to access the text (Erickson & Koppenhaver, 2020). The reading intention can include: predicting or anticipating events; organizing, sequencing, or categorizing the information presented; identifying key characters, plots, or main ideas; making connections within and beyond the text; and summarizing or paraphrasing the information. These reading intentions can be easily connected to grade-level standards and can be used to influence the development of extension activities where students can further apply the information after

TABLE 5.2 Reading Intentions

Reading Intention	Description	Activity example
Making predictions	Predicting or anticipating events that will happen during the story	Before reading, explore book and related materials for the student to share what may happen in the story
Organization	Sequencing or categorizing the information presented	Use the representations from the story (objects, pictures, vocabulary cards) to arrange the aspects of the text to support connections with the story elements
Identifying story elements	Identifying key characters, plots, or main ideas	Use a graphic organizer or story map to record information while the book is being read that can then be used to summarize the text
Applying	Making connections within and beyond the text	Revisit the connections made while activating prior knowledge and predictions made prior to reading
Summarizing	Paraphrasing information using the learner's words and descriptions of the characters, events, and plots described in the text	Have multiple communication modes and digital media available for the student to share their experience of the story

the text has been read. Table 5.2 connects reading intentions to during and after reading activities while also providing examples of related common core standards.

Integrating Comprehension Questions

After a text is read through once, subsequent readings can integrate literal and inferential comprehension questions, with response options connected to the learner's expressive communication abilities and familiar modes (Hudson, 2020). At predetermined locations in the text, alternating sets of comprehension probes can be integrated into each page to cue the adult to ask the question. Questions can be varied and structured to assess content in a variety of ways to prevent memorization and support critical thinking throughout reading. With repeated readings and alternating question sets, varied opportunities to check for understanding will be provided. When asking comprehension questions, modified dialogic reading procedures can be integrated into repeated reading sessions (Whitehurst et al., 1988). Question development can be guided by CROWD+ prompts, which ask a variety of question types (**C**ompletion, **R**ecall, **O**pen-ended, **W**h-, and **D**istancing) that can include specific support strategies, such as additional time for processing, adding binary options (choices and/or yes/no), repeating the prompt, or incorporating individualized supports, such as a token economy or AAC integration (Hudson et al., 2017). See Table 5.3 for examples of CROWD questions that can be integrated into any text, regardless of level or content area.

It is important to remember that the goal is to teach learners how to comprehend the information provided in the text, including strategies for extracting important information from what is being read. Initially, CROWD questions can be integrated into the text in close proximity to where the information is located in the text, such as after a sentence or paragraph. Gradually, questions can be distanced from the material if the learner begins to develop the ability to organize the information obtained from the text, which can be supported with a graphic organizer. Another important consideration is to ensure the learner understands the structure of the questions being asked, which cues the type of response that is expected. For example, a "who" question expects the response to be a person, just like a "where" question expects the response to be a location. Before engaging in interactive reading with a student with extensive support needs, assessment, and if necessary explicit instruction on "Wh-" questions (Who, what, where, when, why, how) may be necessary.

TABLE 5.3 CROWD Prompts

	Description	Question Examples from Ed Roberts: Champion of Disability Rights by Diana Pastora Carson
Completion	Fill-in-the-blank or finishing a phrase or a sentence from the text	An iron lung is a machine Ed Roberts used to help him _____. Ed Roberts was the first person with a significant _____ to attend college at UC Berkeley.
Recall	Inquiring about specific details after a passage is read	What was the main idea of the story? Overall, what did Ed Roberts want to accomplish?
Open-ended	A general question about an aspect of the text	How do you feel about Ed Roberts not being able to go to school? Was Ed Roberts successful in advocating for people with disabilities?
Wh-	Who, what, where, when, why, and how questions	Where did Ed Roberts go to college? Who appointed Ed Roberts as the director of the California Department of Rehabilitation?
Distancing	Questions that connect to concepts or experiences outside of the text	Have you ever advocated for something to change? How does Ed Robert's work connect to Martin Luther King Jr.'s work?

Connection to Lesson Plan

The content covered in this chapter provides information to guide the development of Part D (Table 5.4) of the comprehensive lesson plan. When identifying the prompts that will be incorporated into instruction to support the learner, be sure to indicate the specific prompts and specific details clarifying how each prompt

TABLE 5.4 Part D: Literacy Instruction

Prompting Identify prompts from each level to be used during instruction to support the learner	❑ The learner will **independently** respond without support			
	Auditory	**Visual**		**Tactile**
	❑ General verbal ❑ Specific Verbal	❑ Gestural ❑ Photographic ❑ Model		❑ Partial physical ❑ Full physical
	Prompt detail:			
Target Vocabulary Identify high-utility terms from the text that can be generalized into other contexts and the specific communication mode from Part A that will be used for each to represent each term	**Vocabulary word**			**Representation**
Considerations for vocabulary instruction Ensure that provisions for instruction have been planned for prior to the start of the lesson	❑ Specific communication representations have been identified and created based on individual learner needs ❑ Speech Generating Devices have been programmed and loaded with key vocabulary for each learner ❑ Constant time delay interval has been determined that allows time for the learner to scan available choices and make a selection. Starting time interval: _____ seconds			
Learner attention and prior knowledge	Strategies for securing and maintaining learner attention: Strategies for activating prior knowledge:			

(Cont.)

TABLE 5.4 (Cont.)

Comprehension questions		
Create questions using CROWD+ prompts with varied question styles. Include at least 5 questions in each set that will be alternated during repeated readings of the text.	**LIST A**	**LIST B**
	A1.	B1.
	A2.	B2.
	A3.	B3.
	A4.	B4.
	A5.	B5.
	A6.	B6.

will be delivered. For example, a gestural prompt could indicate pointing to all the available choices or only to the correct answer.

Conclusion

Here are some points to consider when thinking about interactive reading for learners with extensive support needs:

- ♦ Systematic instruction has been proven to be an effective way to teach new skills to learners with extensive support needs. Be sure to understand how the learner demonstrates they are ready to learn and tailor the prompts and time delay interval to meet their specific abilities.
- ♦ Consider teaching high-utility vocabulary words during interactive reading that can be used in other academic situations to support the learner's generalization and overall communication development.

- Teaching emergent literacy skills during interactive reading using the PERM sequence can serve as a natural context to develop skills that will impact the learner's overall engagement with literacy.
- Reading comprehension outcomes can be improved when a specific reading intention is shared with the learner at the start of the activity and comprehension questions are integrated into reading to explicitly teach how and where to locate important information within the text.

References

Alberto, P. A., & Troutman, A. C. (2021). *Applied behavior analysis for teachers* (10th ed.). Pearson.

Beck, I. L., McKeown, M. G., & Kucan, L. (2013). *Bringing words to life: Robust vocabulary instruction* (2nd ed.). Guilford Press.

Browder, D., Ahlgrim-Delzell, L., Spooner, F., Mims, P. J., & Baker, J. N. (2009). Using time delay to teach literacy to students with severe developmental disabilities. *Exceptional Children, 75*(3), 343–364.

Brown, F. E., McDonnell, J., & Snell, M. E. (2019). *Instruction of Students with Severe Disabilities* (9th ed.). Pearson.

Collins, B. C. (2022). *Systematic instruction for students with moderate and severe disabilities* (2nd ed.). Paul H. Brookes Publishing Co.

Copeland, S. R., Head, S. L., & DiLuzio, H. (2018). Getting to the point: Comprehension instruction. In S. R. Copeland & E. B. Keefe (Eds.), *Effective literacy instruction for learners with complex support needs* (2nd ed., pp. 123–149). Paul H. Brookes Publishing Co.

Dessemontet, R. S., Geyer, M., Linder, A. L., Atzemian, M., Martinet, C., Meuli, N., ... & de Chambrier, A. F. (2024). Effects of shared text reading for students with intellectual disability: A meta-analytical review of instructional strategies. *Educational Research Review*, 100615.

Erickson, K. A. (2017). Comprehensive literacy instruction, interprofessional collaborative practice, and students with severe disabilities. *American Journal of Speech-Language Pathology, 26*(2), 193–205.

Erickson, K. A., & Koppenhaver, D. A. (2020). *Comprehensive literacy for all: Teaching students with significant disabilities to read and write*. Paul H. Brookes Publishing Co.

Geist, L., & Erickson, K. (2022). Robust receptive vocabulary instruction for students with significant cognitive disabilities who use AAC. *TEACHING Exceptional Children, 54*(4), 296–304.

Hudson, M. (2020). Teaching English Language Arts standards across the grades. In D. M. Browder, F. Spooner, & G. R. Courtade (Eds.), *Teaching students with moderate and severe disabilities* (2nd ed., pp. 143–159). Guilford Press.

Hudson, R. F., Sanders, E. A., Greenway, R., Xie, S., Smith, M., Gasamis, C., ... & Hackett, J. (2017). Effects of emergent literacy interventions for preschoolers with autism spectrum disorder. *Exceptional children, 84*(1), 55–75.

Joseph, L., Ross, K., Xia, Q., Amspaugh, L. A., & Accurso, J. (2023). Reading comprehension instruction for students with intellectual disabilities: A Systematic literature review. *International Journal of Disability, Development and Education, 70*(3), 314–339.

Kasari, C., Gulsrud, A. C., Shire, S. Y., & Strawbridge, C. (2022). *The Jasper model for children with autism.* Guilford Press.

National Reading Panel. (2000). Report of the National Reading Panel: Teaching children to read—An evidence-based assessment of the scientific research literature on reading and its implications for reading instruction (NIH Pub. No. 00–4769). Washington, DC: U.S. Department of Health and Human Services, Public Health Service, National Institute of Child Health and Human Development.

Orlando, A., & Ruppar, A. (2016). Literacy instruction for students with multiple and severe disabilities who use augmentative/alternative communication (Document No. IC-16). Retrieved from University of Florida, Collaboration for Effective Educator, Development, Accountability, and Reform Center website: http://ceedar.education.ufl.edu/tools/innovation-configurations/

Toews, S. G., McQueston, J., & Kurth, J. A. (2021). Evaluation of the evidence base for shared reading to support literacy skill development for students with extensive support needs. *Research and Practice for Persons with Severe Disabilities, 46*(2), 77–93.

Westling, D. L., Carter, E. W., Da Fonte, M. A., & Kurth, J. A. (2021). *Teaching students with severe disabilities.* Pearson.

Whalon, K., Martinez, J. R., Shannon, D., Butcher, C., & Hanline, M. F. (2015). The impact of reading to engage children with autism in language and learning (RECALL). *Topics in Early Childhood Special Education, 35*(2), 102–115.

Whitehurst, G. J., Falco, F. L., Lonigan, C. J., Fischel, J. E., DeBaryshe, B. D., Valdez-Menchaca, M. C., & Caulfield, M. (1988). Accelerating language development through picture book reading. *Developmental Psychology, 24*(4), 552.

6
Comprehensive Progress Monitoring to Inform Instruction

Teaching aims to use instruction to change the learner's behavior; thus, collecting data during instruction is critical. To track the skills a learner is acquiring, it is important to monitor their progress in a consistent way over time to capture the progression they are making. The data collected needs to be analyzed and interpreted in a way that is meaningful to the teacher and other support personnel, providing an accurate understanding of the skills the learner has achieved. This chapter will explain considerations for progress monitoring during and after instruction. It will also support the development of data collection sheets and analysis that will be used to build complexity for students as they acquire literacy and communication skills during interactive reading.

Instructional Goals and Objectives

Progress monitoring starts with the learning objective that directs what will be taught to the learner. It is important to remember that students demonstrate the skills they have learned through behaviors that others can easily identify. Instructional goals must be observable and measurable and detail the specific behavior

DOI: 10.4324/9781003520030-6

or skill that is expected, the conditions for performance, and the success criteria for mastery (Collins, 2022). Simply stating "the student will understand a story" does not describe the action they will produce to make it clear that the target skill has been acquired. Additionally, IDEA (2004) explains that learning goals and objectives must be related to individual needs and based on academic content standards.

Phases of Learning

When developing instructional goals, it is essential to consider the four phases of learning (acquisition, fluency, maintenance, and generalization) and determine at which phase the learner will be developing their skills (Root et al., 2020). It is essential to provide targeted instruction and assess performance at each phase to ensure progression from acquisition to generalization (Jimenez et al., 2021).

Acquisition

During the acquisition phase of learning, the skill is introduced and cannot be demonstrated reliably without support. This is the starting point of teaching, where new skills are taught. The focus of this stage is building accuracy, which most often involves scaffolding, prompting, and reinforcement. Assessment at the acquisition phase can determine if the learner has the prerequisite skills to eventually perform the behavior independently and how the student responds to instruction. Once a learner begins to demonstrate high levels of accuracy with the skill, requires less scaffolding, and only needs minimal or no prompting, they have most likely moved past the acquisition phase of learning. Learning goals at this phase are focused on the learner having increased support to achieve higher levels of accuracy or moderate accuracy with little to no support. When accuracy is 60% independently or 100% with prompting, the student can progress to the next phase.

Fluency

This phase of learning consists of rate or frequency as well as the accuracy of demonstration of the target behavior. When developing a skill that targets the fluency phase of learning, the individual must be able to demonstrate the skill independently with at least 60% accuracy. The learner has achieved a level of fluency when they are able to perform the skill accurately in a reasonable amount of time. For individuals with extensive support needs, a "reasonable amount of time" means less time than when they first started learning the skill. For example, a student with spastic cerebral palsy may always require additional time to motor plan the movement necessary to activate their communication device, regardless of how fast they can read the word. Learning goals based on fluency must include the rate of demonstration as well as the level of accuracy. To track progress at this stage, data collection can focus on latency (time from request to initiation of skill) or duration (time from start to finish), depending on the skill. The learner has moved beyond the fluency phase once they are able to perform the skill accurately at an appropriate speed with little to no support. Fluency can be attributed to any behavior or skill associated with interactive reading.

Maintenance

Once the learner has acquired the skill and can demonstrate it with 90% accuracy without continuous instruction, they can move into the maintenance phase of learning. This is where they regularly utilize the skill or behavior independently or with very minimal support. Attributes of maintenance include a consistent demonstration of the skill that is self-initiated, independent, and accurate. The learner has achieved skill maintenance once they can demonstrate the skill consistently (e.g., over multiple days), with high accuracy, and at an appropriate rate. Scaffolding and supports, such as prompting, should be faded during this phase. Data collection during the maintenance phase of learning includes accuracy, rate, and number of learning opportunities (trials, days, weeks, etc.) and can be consecutive or non-consecutive, depending on the skill. Assessment probes can be conducted randomly or at predetermined periods. To progress to the next phase, the learner will require opportunities and instruction to demonstrate the behavior or skill outside of the immediate context where it was learned.

Generalization

When the learner can demonstrate the behavior or skill with at least 90% accuracy in a variety of environments with different people and materials, they have entered the generalization phase of learning. Independence is an essential aspect of the generalization phase of learning, as well as the flexibility to adapt the skill to the situation at hand. Periodic skill assessment might be necessary to ensure the learner continues to have the ability to demonstrate the skill. Learning goals for generalization can focus on demonstrating the skill in a different setting, with new people, or using unfamiliar materials. Assessment of generalization can occur when the learner is provided with an ordinary opportunity to demonstrate the skill in a natural setting.

When considering the four phases of learning, initial and ongoing progress monitoring can support teachers in identifying where to begin skill instruction and when to progress to the next phase of learning.

Selecting Behaviors or Skills to Teach

Chapter 3 describes assessment that can be used to identify a learner's literacy and communication skills, which is important to understand before selecting target skills that learning goals will focus on. Target skills consist of either a *discreet behavior* (a single isolated act), such as reading a single word or turning a page of a book, or *chained tasks* (sequenced behaviors that complete a more complex task), such as hand washing or summarizing a passage (Spooner et al., 2012).

When focusing on discreet behavior, the learner's ability is tested through multiple trials or opportunities to demonstrate the skill. For example, if the instructional goal focuses on identifying a sight word during reading, during the interactive reading session, the learner will be provided multiple opportunities to identify the word. For each trial, accuracy and independence are documented so progress can be monitored throughout repeated sessions. A learner may be focusing on multiple discreet behaviors or skills at one time.

Chained tasks are more complex, and each step or discreet behavior involved can be analyzed regardless of whether the intended outcome was achieved. For example, demonstrating proper book handling while reading. For students with extensive support needs, a task analysis can be a useful tool to break down the discreet behaviors that comprise the chained task so that each step can be assessed (McConomy et al., 2021).

The steps for developing a task analysis include:

1. Observe a task that peers are performing and record the discreet behaviors the student is expected to demonstrate.
2. Create a list of the steps in the process based on the observed discreet behaviors where each step builds upon and reinforces the previous step.
3. Develop each step in the task analysis based on student abilities and required areas of support, the environment where the activity will occur, and the learner's communication needs (including the level of symbolic understanding, as well as receptive and expressive communication forms). Ensure the activity is accessible to the student across visual and auditory sensory channels and incorporate necessary accommodations.
4. Incorporate a system of least-to-most prompts to support the learner and determine the specific types of prompts to be used across visual, auditory, and tactile channels.
5. Utilize explicit instruction to model and teach the learner how to use the task analysis to complete the chained behavior. Update the talk analysis as needed to reflect added modifications and accommodations that may be identified when teaching the steps.
6. Monitor and assess the learner's progress and support required at each step, such as the level of prompting that was needed to demonstrate each discreet behavior. Continue to revise the steps as needed based on observation and analysis of the learner's performance.

> **Example of a Chained Task**
>
> Instructional Goal: When presented with a book before an interactive reading session, the student will demonstrate proper book-handling skills while the book is read with 100% accuracy.
> Step 1: Select a book from the classroom library and bring it to the reading area
> Step 2: Correctly orient the book
> Step 3: Read the title of the book
> Step 4: Read the author's name
> Step 5: Gently open the cover to the first page of the story
> Step 6: After each page is read, gently turn the page
> Step 7: When the book is finished, close the cover and reorient the book
> Step 8: Return the book to the classroom library

Writing High-Quality Learning Goals

Starting with an understanding of the learner's current abilities and needs, all learning goals follow a similar structure of condition, learner, behavior, and criteria, regardless of whether these goals are included in the learner's IEP (Hedin & DeSpain, 2018). Additionally, short-term objectives can also be included to ensure progress monitoring for all aspects of the learner's skill development.

Guidance is available to develop learning goals that are specific, observable, and measurable (Goran et al., 2020). This includes developing learning goals that are:

1. **Simple, clear, and easily understood.** This includes writing goals that do not include jargon, acronyms, or technical language. Goals should be concise and written so that what is being measured can be easily understood by most people. Avoid long and complex goals that are highly technical and measure the progression of multiple skills.
2. **Focus on student behaviors.** Students demonstrate understanding and learning through behaviors. Learning goals should be focused on the learner producing an explicit action that can be easily observed by others rather than teacher actions to elicit a skill demonstration.

3. **Address areas for skill development identified from assessment.** Prior to developing learning goals, conducting a baseline assessment can ensure that the instructional targets being established are aligned with the learner's current level of performance.
4. **Communicate intention.** Characteristics of intentional learning goals include a target skill that the student is expected to demonstrate, conditions and context for performing the behavior, criteria for success and level of proficiency, and an expected timeline of progress for mastery.
5. **Include a suitable level of rigor.** Learning targets should be individualized, meaningful, and appropriately challenging to the learner and consider the results of the baseline assessment(s), their abilities and areas that require support, and connected to their educational needs.

Checklist for Developing Learning Goals for Students with Extensive Support Needs

(Adapted from Hedin & DeSpain, 2018)
The learning goal is:

- ❏ Free from jargon, acronyms, or technical language and can be easily understood by someone outside of education
- ❏ Focuses on a single target skill or behavior that is easily observable and measurable that was identified through baseline assessment(s)
- ❏ Describes conditions and context for performance, including activity and materials if appropriate
- ❏ Includes success criteria, as well as supports, modification, and adaptations the learner requires
- ❏ Aligns with a realistic anticipated level of proficiency based on baseline assessment(s) and a familiar understanding of the student
- ❏ Incorporates time periods for each specific learning objective (if included), individual learning trials, and anticipated completion.

Using Data to Inform Instruction

Data-based decision-making is a useful practice for all teachers, including for those implementing instruction for students with extensive support needs (Ruhter & Karvonen, 2024). It is an evidence-based practice where teachers collect, analyze, and

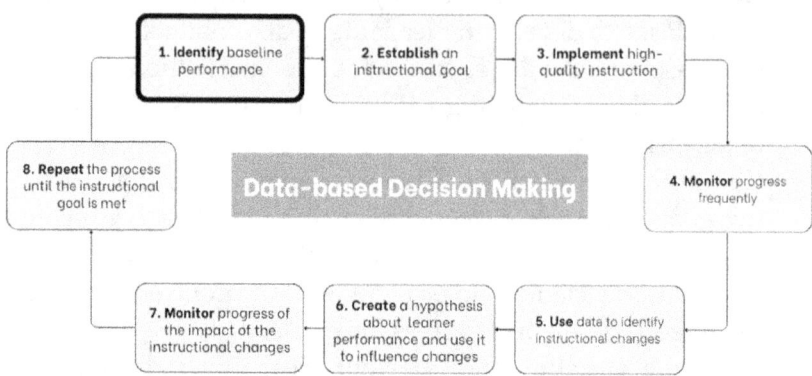

FIGURE 6.1 Data-based decision-making process

interpret student performance data to influence the instructional decisions they make (Jung et al., 2018).

Although there are slight variations, the overall steps to data-based decision-making typically involve a structured process for analyzing progress monitoring data, which can be seen in Figure 6.1. Progress monitoring in the form of data collection is a critical aspect of data-based decision-*making*; however, teachers can often find data collection and analysis a challenge (Ruble et al., 2018). Utilizing a team-based approach to decision-making by including members of the multidisciplinary team and families can provide comprehensive insight into the effectiveness of the instructional procedures that are implemented and the supports being provided. Literacy skills that support interactive reading can be developed outside of the activity with related service personnel. For example, the speech-language pathologist can work teaching the learner to use their speech-generating device (SGD) to access vocabulary from the text and collect data on the learner's performance. Related service providers can also support data collection during instruction, especially if working one-on-one with a student during the interactive lesson. Once the learning goal has been established, collaborative data collection can begin.

Data Collection

Regardless of the learning stage, a data collection system is necessary to capture situational information and performance data and to summarize the information collected (Collins, 2022). The system can be as simple as marking ticks on scrap paper or include detailed data collection sheets; regardless of the collection style, certain information must be collected. Situational information is the contextual information that helps explain the conditions under which the data was collected. This includes the student's name, the person collecting the data, the date, time of day, target skill, setting, and any other pertinent information that would be helpful to better understand the information collected, such as the phase of learning, reinforcement provided, etc. Performance data is the heart of the data collection sheet. This is where the learner's performance is recorded for each trial, whether the instructional goal focuses on a discreet behavior or a chained task. Key considerations for developing a system to collect this information include how to capture the accuracy of the responses (accurate, inaccurate, and failure to respond) as well as the level of independence the learner exhibited for each trial or step. Lastly, summary data provides a brief description of the information that was collected. This can be as simple as a total number of correct responses or a number of trials where the learner required prompts to produce an accurate response. The key is that the summary data is easily calculated and explains, either in a very simple or highly complex manner, the student's performance.

Before beginning instruction, it is important to collect baseline data by observing the learner's ability to perform the skill using the same instructional materials (Westling et al., 2021). Instruction is not to occur during baseline data collection, as the intention is to obtain an understanding of the learner's abilities and be sure they do not have the ability to perform the skills. Observation during baseline can also help to identify additional adaptations needed to the materials or environmental supports that need to be implemented. For example, during a baseline observation, the observer may notice that the learner's visual access to the book is impeded due to glare on the book's laminated pages. Noticing this can allow for a non-laminated copy to be used or for the book to be positioned on a slant board in front of the student.

When collecting instructional data during interactive reading, it is important to collect performance data that reflect the accuracy and level of independence for each discreet behavior (e.g., vocabulary words and comprehension questions). Simply stating the number correct does not provide sufficient information on where the student is specifically struggling. For example, the learner could be struggling to understand a specific vocabulary word or not be able to answer a certain type of comprehension question. In this case, more information can direct the teacher to provide additional targeted instruction to support the acquisition of these skills.

Figure 6.2 provides an example of a completed data sheet used for interactive reading that provides detailed information on accuracy and independence for vocabulary learning. A template of the form is provided in Appendix B. The data sheet allows for accuracy and level of independence to be recorded for each vocabulary word and comprehension question. After a given trial, the number of accurate items is circled for the vocabulary and comprehension questions. Depending on the learner's instructional goals, this can be the number of items that were answered accurately independently or with prompting. Regardless of whether supported trials are included in the total number, it is important for the scorer to remain consistent when summarizing the information. After multiple trials, the scorer can connect the circled items to easily create a graph that can display progress over time. If using alternating sets of comprehension questions, different colors can be used to track progress for sets A and B, as shown in the example.

Emergent literacy skills can be taught as individual discreet behaviors or as a chained task. When teaching the skills as discreet behaviors, data collection can be conducted in the same manner that was demonstrated for vocabulary and comprehension. This allows for each skill to be developed individually. However, emergent literacy skills can also be looked at as chained tasks, as noted in the example provided above. After a task analysis has been conducted, the steps involved are listed on the data sheet. Table 6.1 provides an example of a data collection

Interactive Reading Data Collection Sheet

Student: Macey G.		Dates: Oct. 26	
Scorer: SPED teacher	Title: Ed Roberts: Champion of Disability Rights		Location: Classroom (1:1)

Scoring: List the word or comprehension question on the designated list. At the start of the trial, enter the data at the top of the column. For each item, indicate the accuracy on the left side of the cell and level of independence or prompt provided on the right side.

Accuracy: ✗ correct and independent | **Prompt level:** A – auditory V – visual T – tactile

Words	1	2	3	4	5	6	7	8	9	10
access	✗|T	✗|T	✗|T	✗|V	✗|V	✗|V	✗|V	✗|A	✗|A	✗|A
advocate	✗|T	✗|T	✗|V	✗|T	✗|V	✗|V	✗|V	✗|V	✗|A	✗|A
college	✗|V	✗|A	✗|A	✗|A	✗|A	✗|A	✗|A	✗|A	✗|	✗|
diploma	✗|	✗|	✗|	✗|	✗|	✗|	✗|	✗|	✗|	✗|
disability	✗|A	✗|	✗|A	✗|	✗|	✗|	✗|	✗|	✗|	✗|
equality	✗|T	✗|V	✗|V	✗|V	✗|V	✗|A	✗|A	✗|A	✗|A	✗|A
graduated	✗|V	✗|A	✗|A	✗|	✗|	✗|	✗|	✗|	✗|	✗|
laws	✗|V	✗|V	✗|V	✗|A	✗|	✗|A	✗|	✗|	✗|	✗|
Graphing Circle the total number of correct and independent trials for each session then graph across all sessions.	8 7 6 5 4 3 2 1	8 7 6 5 4 3 2 1	8 7 6 5 4 3 2 1	8 7 6 5 4 3 2 1	8 7 6 5 4 3 2 1	8 7 6 5 4 3 2 1	8 7 6 5 4 3 2 1	8 7 6 5 4 3 2 1	8 7 6 5 4 3 2 1	8 7 6 5 4 3 2 1

FIGURE 6.2 Example of completed data collection sheet for vocabulary learning

TABLE 6.1 Data Collection Sheet for Chained Emergent Literacy Skills

Scoring: For each item, indicate the accuracy on the left side of the cell and level of independence or prompt provided on the right side.						
Accuracy: ✓ correct ✗ incorrect | **Independence**: I – independent A – auditory V – visual T – tactile						
Procedure	Criteria	1	2	3	4	5
Step 1: Select a book from the classroom library and bring it to the reading area						
Step 2: Correctly orient the book						
Step 3: As the adult points to the title of the book, use SGD to state "title"						
Step 4: As the adult points to the author of the book, use SGD to state "author"						
Step 5: Gently open the cover to the first page of the story						
Step 6: After each page is read, gently turn the page or use SGD to state, "turn the page"						
Step 7: When the book is finished, close the cover and reorient the book						
Step 8: Return the book to its original location						

sheet that could be developed for chained emergent literacy skills for a learner using an SGD to communicate.

Data-Based Decision Making

After enough performance data has been collected and graphed, it is time to inspect the data to identify patterns or trends in the data that can provide insight into the learner's literacy skill acquisition and guide instructional changes (Filderman et al., 2018). This process includes using an analysis of the data to influence an instructional decision and implementing the change in programming. For example, if a student is not making adequate progress toward learning the steps of a chained task, a change to improve success may be to decrease the number of discreet behaviors that are included in the sequence.

Using the graphs produced by the data sheets shown above can make identifying trends easier to identify with minimal effort. First, visual analysis can be used to see if the graph is trending upward to indicate an increase in accuracy. It is also important to note if the accuracy is independently achieved or accomplished with the support of prompting. Conversely, the data may show a lack of progress, indicating that a change in skill focus may be necessary by possibly decreasing the number of steps in the task analysis or revisiting a preceding skill. If visual inspection does not provide a clear understanding, further analysis may be required. First, using the most recent month of data, the mean performance can be calculated and compared to the initial two-week period and the most recent two-week period. Comparing the means can demonstrate progress if the most recent measure is at least 5% higher than the initial measure. Once the data has been analyzed and progress identified, instructional changes can be made and implemented.

Instructional Changes and Building Complexity

Instructional decision rules can guide teachers in either simplifying or building complexity with their instruction (Pennington, 2020). After data has been analyzed, the emerging patterns and trends can be used to guide adjustments to the instructional program. Table 6.2 provides guidance for interpreting data to make informed instructional decisions. When considering implementing changes, it is important to change only one aspect of the instructional program at a time and continue to collect and analyze learner performance data to identify the impact of the changes made. Additionally, the new modification needs time to work, so be sure to implement it long enough for change to occur.

It is important to note that support provided during an intervention cannot simply end once a new skill or discreet behavior is independently demonstrated. Instead, the supports must be systematically faded (Estrapala et al., 2018). This includes scaffolding, such as prompting and reinforcement for correct responses. While systematically fading supports to increase independence, data collection must not be disrupted so that progress can be continuously monitored to identify the key components of the intervention that are sustaining learner success. It is important to also remember that certain supports are essential for learner access, and diminishing them would impose access barriers for the

TABLE 6.2 Data-based Decision Making

Data trend	Regression	No progress	Slow progress	Rapid progress
Focus	**Adjust reinforcement and motivate participation**	**Simplify instruction to be more accessible to the learner**	**Implement instructional adjustment to prompting hierarchy and stimulus presentation**	**Build complexity, maximize independence, and promote skill maintenance and generalization**
Suggested strategies	Positively reinforce accurate and independent responses with tangible items/activities that are highly preferred	Streamline the task analysis by breaking down the chained task into smaller steps or teach steps in segments	Reduce prompting to a minimal level, and increase time delay interval before a prompt is provided	Increase rigor with more complex communication representations or more sophisticated question types
	Incorporate choice and variety into the activity, allowing the student to choose materials or number of items to complete	Simplify response methods by reducing the cognitive and motor demand (e.g., by reducing the field of choice or replace a manual sign with pointing)	Implement graduated guidance to use lesser intrusive prompts and fading the amount of tactile support (as much as possible)	Remove all prompting supports and reinforce independent responses
	Ignore errors and implement natural consequences	Manipulate or change the materials to increase the likelihood of a correct response	Assess the learner's proximity to the materials to ensure optimal visual, auditory, and tactile access	Encourage skill demonstration with new materials, people, or environments
	Fade prompts and only reinforce accurate responses	Incorporate assistive technology to support material access, communication, and position	Incorporate self-guidance by implementing a video model or visual activity schedule	Incorporate extension activities that require summarizing and synthesizing information
	Increase data collection efforts	Assess the materials and environment and limit or remove potential barriers or ambient distractions	Model responses and incorporate peers and other staff members into the activity	Promote spontaneous skill demonstration in natural situations and in unfamiliar environments

Adapted from Pennington (2020).

learner. This includes supports for visual, auditory, and tactile access, as well as mobility considerations, such as increased time for motor planning and augmentative and alternative communication supports. Conversely, once the learner has reached an optimal level of independence that includes their necessary support, building complexity can sustain higher phases of learning and support the development of more complex skills. For example, during vocabulary instruction, the adult can increase the sophistication of the supplementary supports (e.g., use pictures instead of objects) or gradually remove them altogether. During shared reading, complexity can be supported by utilizing comprehension probes from the later end of the CROWD sequence (i.e., open-ended, wh-questions, and distancing) and removing any additional supports.

Conclusion

Here are some points to consider when thinking about progress monitoring to inform instruction for learners with extensive support needs:

- ♦ Assessment drives instruction. It is important to understand the student's current phase of learning related to the target skill before developing a learning goal for instruction.
- ♦ A task analysis can be a successful way to teach any chained task; however, when developing each step, be sure to consider the learner's abilities and how additional support can be provided to support their success. Some steps may require more support than others to achieve the desired outcome.
- ♦ A successful data collection system is one that is consistently used to monitor student progress. If a system is too complex, it is less likely it will be correctly implemented by all members of the student's team. Simple learning goals can drive simple and very effective data collection systems.

References

Collins, B. C. (2022). *Systematic instruction for students with moderate and severe disabilities* (2nd ed.). Paul H. Brookes Publishing Co.

Estrapala, S., Rila, A., & Bruhn, A. L. (2018). Don't quit cold turkey: Systematic fading to promote sustained behavioral change. *TEACHING Exceptional Children, 51*(1), 54–61.

Filderman, M. J., Toste, J. R., Didion, L. A., Peng, P., & Clemens, N. H. (2018). Data-based decision making in reading interventions: A synthesis and meta-analysis of the effects for struggling readers. *The Journal of Special Education, 52*(3), 174–187.

Goran, L., Harkins Monaco, E. A., Yell, M. L., Shriner, J., & Bateman, D. (2020). Pursuing Academic and Functional Advancement: Goals, Services, and Measuring Progress. *TEACHING Exceptional Children, 52*(5), 333-343. https://doi.org/10.1177/0040059920919924

Hedin, L., & DeSpain, S. (2018). Smart or not: Writing specific, measurable IEP goals. *TEACHING Exceptional Children, 51*(2), 100–110.

Individuals with Disabilities Education Act, 20 U.S.C. § 1400 (2004).

Jimenez, B., Root, J., & Bouck, E. C. (2021). Using the four stages of learning to assess, set goals, and instruct. *TEACHING Exceptional Children, 56*(6), 452–461.

Jung, P.-G., McMaster, K. L., Kunkel, A. K., Shin, J., & Stecker, P. M. (2018). Effects of data-based individualization for students with intensive learning needs: A meta-analysis. *Learning Disabilities Research & Practice, 33*(3), 144–155.

McConomy, M. A., Root, J., & Wade, T. (2021). Using task analysis to support inclusion and assessment in the classroom. *TEACHING Exceptional Children, 54*(6), 414–422.

Pennington, R. (2020). Monitoring and enhancing student progress. In D. M. Browder, F. Spooner, & G. R. Courtade (Eds.), *Teaching students with moderate and severe disabilities* (2nd ed., pp. 93–113). Guilford Press.

Root, J. R., Wood, L., & Browder, D. M. (2020). Assessment and planning. In F. Brown, J. McDonnell, & M. E. Snell (Eds.), *Instruction of students with severe disabilities* (2nd ed., pp. 60–96). Pearson.

Ruble, L. A., McGrew, J. H., Wong, W. H., & Missall, K. N. (2018). Special education teachers' perceptions and intentions toward data collection. *Journal of Early Intervention, 40*(2), 177–191.

Ruhter, L., & Karvonen, M. (2024). The impact of professional development on data-based decision-making for students with extensive support needs. *Remedial and Special Education, 45*(1), 44–57.

Spooner, F., Knight, V. F., Browder, D. M., & Smith, B. R. (2012). Evidence-based practice for teaching academics to students with severe developmental disabilities. *Remedial and Special Education, 33*(6), 374–387.

Westling, D. L., Carter, E. W., Da Fonte, M. A., & Kurth, J. A. (2021). *Teaching students with severe disabilities* (6th ed.). Pearson.

7

Developing and Sustaining Opportunities for Inclusion

Inclusive education settings have many social and educational benefits for all learners, especially for those with extensive support needs, when provided with high-quality instruction that includes individualized supports (Westling et al., 2021). In recent years, research on inclusive practices has focused on integrating instruction for learners with extensive support needs into general education and other settings by utilizing systematic instruction, integrated peer supports, and universal design for learning (Kuntz & Carter, 2019). For students with disabilities, inclusion in general education has been identified as a predictor of post-secondary success (Mazzotti et al., 2016).

Engaging in inclusive practices also has social benefits for learners with and without disabilities. For learners with extensive support needs, this includes opportunities to develop relationships with peers with disabilities that can have long-lasting positive impacts on communication skills, social interactions, perceptions of belonging, standards for achievement, and overall quality of life (Wehmeyer et al., 2021). Relatedly, for students without disabilities, the benefits of learning alongside a peer with extensive support needs can be reciprocal, including improved social interactions, increased understanding of persons with disabilities, improved attitudes, and improved advocacy skills

DOI: 10.4324/9781003520030-7

(Travers & Carter, 2022). However, inclusion can often be challenging to implement, and learners with extensive support needs who use augmentative and alternative communication (AAC) may have difficulties communicating and interacting with peers within general education environments (Ballard & Dymond, 2017).

Successful Inclusion

Conceptual frameworks exist to structure and guide the inclusion of learners with disabilities into general education settings. These frameworks integrate accommodations and other supports so that all students can access the general education curriculum, including universal design for learning, opportunities to learn, and other evidence-based practices such as collaborative teaming and peer-mediated instruction (Ryndak et al., 2020).

Universal Design for Learning

As mentioned in Chapter 3, universal design for learning (UDL) is a framework for designing curricula to support all learners from the start rather than retrofitting modifications and accommodations later (Rose, 2000). The UDL framework outlines a structure for providing multiple means of engagement, multiple means of representation, and multiple opportunities for action and expression so that all learners can make meaningful progress (CAST, 2024). This includes integrating flexible formats into the instructional goals, curricular materials, and assessment methods used in the classroom, often including digital media and technology to accommodate the learning styles and needs of a wide range of students. The UDL framework encourages the digitization of written text and further enhancement of static materials by adding supplementary audio and video, as well as providing additional visuals and other supports to organize information like graphic organizers and story maps. Assessment is also enhanced to cross different modes and create new and diverse opportunities for students to demonstrate the information they have learned.

Collaborative Teaming

As mentioned in previous chapters, when planning any instruction for learners with extensive support needs, it is essential for special education teachers to collaborate with families and other school professionals to ensure the learner's complex needs are being appropriately supported. Collaborative teaming has been shown to increase outcomes related to engagement, academic progress, and social interactions for learners with extensive support needs using AAC (Biggs et al., 2017). The model includes utilizing the learner's IEP team to monitor and create necessary instructional supports for the student to access the general education curriculum, promote independence, and design and implement accommodations and modifications. Team members include school personnel who provide ongoing support for the learner's instructional needs, such as the special and general educators, families, and related service personnel who are familiar with the students and provide services as IEP team members. The collaborative team can be effective in developing curricular plans and necessary accommodations for inclusion in general education, identifying and assessing communication needs and developing AAC systems, identifying technology supports for the learner, fostering and facilitating peer relationships, and promoting inclusion to the maximum extent possible (Westling et al., 2021).

Peer-Mediated Supports

There are different approaches for using peers to support learners with extensive support needs within general education settings. Programs can support the development of peer relationships and help learners with extensive support needs access the benefits of learning with peers without disabilities. A school's structure and commitment to inclusion may make it easier to adopt one of the programs over the others. When selecting a peer-mediated program that focuses on learning academic content, peer support arrangements enhance inclusive education by having one or more peers without disabilities provide social and academic support to a learner with extensive support needs (Carter, 2018). Before starting, special education teachers plan how the learner with extensive support needs will access instruction within the general education classroom and how support will be provided for social and academic interactions by the peer and other instructional staff (teachers, paraprofessionals, related service, etc.). The supporting peers then receive training on the learner's specific needs and how to implement supports to facilitate interactions and meaningful access to the content. This also includes training on how the learner uses their AAC device for expressive communication and other strategies to support effective communication exchanges. For academic work, the learner and peer can collaborate on assignments, participate in group discussions, or share materials. Initially, a paraprofessional may also directly support the learner and the peer partner. However, this can be faded to encourage richer interactions between the learner and the peer. If the learner has medical or other complex support needs, the paraprofessional will remain within the general education setting but provide more general support to the class and be available if needed.

Peer-mediated interventions can effectively support inclusion. The learner with extensive support needs receives support from their peer partner through social interactions that help them further develop their communication skills, learn grade-level academic content, and interact meaningfully with their peers. The peer's initial and ongoing training equips them to support the learner, and the presence of the paraprofessional provides additional security, with further assistance readily available. School teams, with support from administrators, can develop plans to develop and maintain a peer support program for their learners with extensive support needs (Carter et al., 2015). Planning how inclusion will be facilitated and how the learner will be supported by their peer and the paraprofessional outside of the special education classroom is essential. The steps for establishing a peer support program include the following:

1. **Create a plan.** Determine how school personnel and peers will collaborate to support the learner's participation in instructional activities, with detailed information on the types of support the peer is expected to provide and how the paraprofessional and general education teacher will work together. This requires observations in the general education classroom to identify how the learner with extensive support needs can participate authentically and interact socially within the setting. Additionally, when planning the activity, conversations between the general and special education teachers are necessary to discuss materials, access to the instruction, and specific accommodations and modifications that may be necessary.
2. **Identify a peer.** It is critical to select peers to support the learner who is motivated to build a relationship with the learner and support them as needed within the general education classroom. Ideally, peers with an interest in special education or experience working with individuals with extensive support needs are optimal candidates; however, peers with aligning interests or who are curious to learn how to support an individual with extensive needs should also be considered.
3. **Hold a peer orientation meeting.** Initial and ongoing training should provide an overview of the program, background information on the learner (interests, strengths, communication modes, etc.), and general participation expectations. Information on providing instructional and communication support, as well as how and when to seek the assistance of the paraprofessional, is also important. This meeting should also provide an opportunity for the peer to ask questions and for the special educator to address any hesitations or concerns.
4. **Begin the program.** After the orientation meeting, the peer can be introduced to the learner and start working together. At first, the paraprofessional can remain close by and model effective instructional and communication support for the peer to utilize. Over time, the paraprofessional will gradually fade their involvement but still remain within the general education classroom and monitor from a distance.

Planning for Inclusion

When implementing a high-quality inclusive experience for learners with extensive support needs, it is important to use the recommended frameworks (UDL and OTL) and evidence-based practices (collaborative teaming and peer-mediated instruction) to develop meaningful opportunities for social and learning interactions with their peers. However, with so many factors involved, it can become overwhelming trying to ensure all the essential aspects are present to make the experience successful. Inclusive education experiences for learners with extensive support needs can be systematically planned when curricular adaptations and supports for instruction and participation are collaboratively planned (Thompson et al., 2018). Together, the general and special education teachers can begin to plan the curriculum, supports, and opportunities for interaction to provide a high-quality and meaningful experience for the learner with extensive support needs and their peers (Carpenter et al., 2023). Table 7.1 provides considerations and guiding questions to consider when planning inclusive opportunities for learners with extensive support needs.

Aided AAC Modeling

Aided AAC modeling describes the process of providing language modeling to an individual using speech or their AAC system. A peer can utilize the learner's AAC system (or a parallel version) during interactions to model communication throughout a learning activity. When effectively integrated into a peer support program, peer-implemented AAC modeling can improve symbolic communication and positive social interactions with peers for learners with extensive support needs (Biggs et al., 2018). Working together also improves the social experience for the peer and the learner while also serving as a model for other students within the general education setting to interact with the learner. When using aided AAC modeling with peers, participation from the collaborative team is important to provide support for the learner's positioning, vocabulary, device programming,

TABLE 7.1 Planning Considerations for Meaningful Inclusion

Considerations for support	*Guiding questions*
Curricular adaptations focus on modifying the general education content so that it is appropriate for the learner's abilities and areas that require support. This can include providing additional content, modifying content to better align with the learner's abilities, or providing similar and related content that can be taught with the general content.	What is the overall learning goal for the lesson? Will the learning goal need to be modified for the learner with extensive support to meaningfully participate in the lesson? Would an alternative learning goal for the learner increase their access to the content and facilitate higher-quality interactions with peers?
Instructional supports focus on the instructional strategies and materials that are utilized within the general education classroom. Planning instructional strategies includes identifying the activity that will take place and determine how the learner will participate, including whether individualized strategies are necessary to appropriately support the learner.	Does the learner require additional instruction or accommodations to meet the learning goal for the lesson? What accommodations are needed to ensure the learner can authentically engage with the content during the lesson?
Participation supports include individualized and intentional provisions for the learner to have meaningful interaction and engagement within the general education classroom. This may include peer-mediated supports, communication supports, and the integration of assistive technology. This also includes considering the routine of the general education classroom, including transition times, less structured times, and opportunities for social engagement with peers.	What supports for participation are needed ensure communicative interactions with peers? Are the peers in the classroom familiar with the learner's communication system, including the expressive communication forms they frequently utilize?

assess the impact of the intervention, and provide support to the peer as needed (Kleinert et al., 2023). The input from the paraprofessional providing support within the general education classroom is also important to obtain a hands-on perspective of the intervention.

Supporting Inclusion During Literacy Instruction

In general, literacy can be an effective time to include a learner with extensive support needs in a general education setting. This includes including learners in grade-level literacy instruction. Augmenting literacy activities can facilitate access for the learner and provide them the opportunity to learn alongside and interact with their peers. When the content within the general education classroom may not be accessible to the learner with extensive support needs, curricular changes can be made to enhance the learner's experience with inclusion (Thompson et al., 2018). This includes supplementing the content of the lesson with related information, modifying the content to reflect a difficulty level that is accessible, or providing alternate content that can be taught to the learner alongside their peers. Table 7.2 provides a guide for planning inclusive literacy experiences for learners with extensive support needs. When using the guide, it is important to maintain an understanding of the specific supports the learner may require for access to the materials and the learning environment, including access to visual, auditory, and tactile information, as well as physical access to areas of the classroom.

Conclusion

Here are some points to consider when thinking about inclusion for learners with extensive support needs:

- Successful inclusion takes careful planning and support from a variety of sources. Be sure to include the general education teacher, paraprofessionals, and IEP team members when planning inclusion efforts to ensure the learner's needs are fully supported.

TABLE 7.2 Planning Inclusive Literacy Experiences

Components	Considerations
Types of Learning Opportunities	
Learning activities scheduled as a part of the classroom routine	Review how the learner will access and participate in classroom routines, considering the communication expectations, classroom rules and norms, and schedule of activities. Remember to include provisions for self-care such as bathroom needs and breaks.
Transitions, free time, or less structured class times	What are the expectations for the learner during less-structured classroom times and will they require additional adult support?
Planning and Instruction	
Material preparation	Adapt and modify texts as needed to accommodate the individual needs of the learner. Prepare AAC device by programming and pre-teaching vocabulary related to the activity.
Environmental arrangement	Ensure the learner has physical access to all learning spaces. Include specialized positioning and mobility equipment, as needed, and rearrange furniture to increase the learner's ability to easily move around the classroom.
Skill acquisition	Pre-teach content beforehand to better equip the learner to follow along during instruction and participate in discussions and related activities.
Generalization and maintenance	Identify skills that can be generalized into general education. For example, how will the student seek the attention of the teacher? (E.g., raising hand? Using AAC device?)
Data collection and monitoring	Develop and implement data collection procedures, including what data will be collected, how frequently, and by whom. Have data collection materials available.
Support Providers	
Peers	Provide training and pre-instruction to peers on the expectations for providing support, content of the activity, and expected performance and participation outcomes for the learner.
Paraprofessional	Review expectations for support to be provided within the general education classroom and at what distance. Identify key information to be articulated to the general education teacher during and after the lesson, as well as information to be shared after with the special education teacher.
General and special education teachers	Hold advance-planning conversations regarding the content of the lesson and the activities to explore how the learner will continue to be meaningfully engaged throughout the lesson and have authentic opportunities to participate and interact with peers.

Adapted from Ruppar (2013).

- Preparing for inclusion also involves curriculum planning. Utilizing UDL to guide planning instruction can support a variety of learning styles and needs by providing options. Considering inclusion from the beginning means options can be integrated into instruction from the start rather than being added as an afterthought.
- Engaging peers when planning and implementing inclusion benefits everyone. They can provide academic support, model AAC use, and elicit opportunities for interaction and participation while also potentially becoming friends.

References

Ballard, S. L., & Dymond, S. K. (2017). Addressing the general education curriculum in general education settings with students with severe disabilities. *Research and Practice for Persons with Severe Disabilities*, 42(3), 155–170.

Biggs, E. E., Carter, E. W., & Gustafson, J. (2017). Efficacy of peer support arrangements to increase peer interaction and AAC use. *American Journal on Intellectual and Developmental Disabilities*, 122(1), 25–48.

Biggs, E. E., Carter, E. W., Bumble, J. L., Barnes, K., & Mazur, E. L. (2018). Enhancing peer network interventions for students with complex communication needs. *Exceptional Children*, 85(1), 66–85.

Carpenter, M. E., Walker, V. L., Fredrick, D., & Edyburn, D. L. (2023). Systematically planning supports to promote access to and meaningful participation in general education settings for students with IDD. *Teaching Exceptional Children*, 56(2), 90–97.

Carter, E. W. (2018). Supporting the social lives of secondary students with severe disabilities: Considerations for effective intervention. *Journal of Emotional and Behavioral Disorders*, 26(1), 52–61.

Carter, E. W., Moss, C. K., Asmus, J., Fesperman, E., Cooney, M., Brock, M. E., Lyons, G., Huber, H. B., & Vincent, L. B. (2015). Promoting inclusion, social connections, and learning through peer support arrangements. *Teaching Exceptional Children*, 48(1), 9–18.

CAST. (2024). *Universal Design for Learning Guidelines* (Version 3.0). Retrieved from http://udlguidelines.cast.org

Kleinert, H. L., Kearns, J., Land, L. A., Page, J. L., & Kleinert, J. O. R. (2023). Peer-assisted aided AAC modeling for students with complex communication needs. *Teaching Exceptional Children, 55*(4), 268–277.

Kuntz, E. M., & Carter, E. W. (2019). Review of interventions supporting secondary students with intellectual disability in general education classes. *Research and Practice for Persons with Severe Disabilities, 44*(2), 103–121.

Mazzotti, V. L., Rowe, D. A., Sinclair, J., Poppen, M., Woods, W. E., & Shearer, M. L. (2016). Predictors of post-school success: A systematic review of NLTS2 secondary analyses. *Career Development and Transition for Exceptional Individuals, 39*(4), 196–215.

Rose, D. (2000). Universal design for learning. *Journal of Special Education Technology, 15*(4), 47–51.

Ruppar, A. L. (2013). Authentic literacy and communication in inclusive settings for students with significant disabilities. *Teaching Exceptional Children, 46*(2), 44–50.

Ryndak, D. L., Orlando, A., & Burnette, K. K. (2020). Creating and implementing inclusive education. In F. Brown, J. McDonnell, & M. E. Snell (Eds.), *Instruction of students with severe disabilities* (2nd ed., pp. 207–231). Pearson.

Thompson, J. R., Walker, V. L., Shogren, K. A., & Wehmeyer, M. L. (2018). Expanding inclusive educational opportunities for students with the most significant cognitive disabilities through personalized supports. *Intellectual and Developmental Disabilities, 56*(6), 396–411.

Travers, H. E., & Carter, E. W. (2022). A systematic review of how peer-mediated interventions impact students without disabilities. *Remedial and Special Education, 43*(1), 40–57.

Wehmeyer, M. L., Shogren, K. A., & Kurth, J. (2021). The state of inclusion with students with intellectual and developmental disabilities in the United States. *Journal of Policy and Practice in Intellectual Disabilities, 18*(1), 36–43.

Westling, D. L., Carter, E. W., Da Fonte, M. A., & Kurth, J. A. (2021). *Teaching students with severe disabilities* (6th ed.). Pearson.

Appendix A
Comprehensive Lesson Planning Template

Student Name:	Date:
Age:	Grade-level:

Part A: Learner Assets and Areas of Support	
Personal Characteristics: Assess strengths and weaknesses in functioning, including areas of strength and necessary supports. Utilize the information covered and assessment resources from Chapters 2 and 3 to complete this section. Additionally, consultation with relevant related service personnel (SLP, OT, PT, TVI, TOD, COMS, etc.) is recommended.	
Background and Culture Aspects of the learner's history, background, and previous experiences that contribute to their identity	Diagnosis, medical history, and current health status: Culture: Family life and language at home: Interests:
Sensory Abilities Results from formal, informal, and functional assessments that demonstrate how information is received from each sensory channel	Vision: Hearing: Tactile: Learning media:
Motor Abilities Consider range of motion, strength, tone, and extent of voluntary control, as well as current equipment and positioning supports that are needed for optimal access to instruction and the learning environment	Fine motor: Gross motor: Adaptive equipment and positioning:

Communication Describe the complexity of the learner's communication modes, as well as supports they require (tangible symbols, speech-generating device, communication board, etc.)	Receptive communication modes: Expressive communication modes: Augmentative and alternative communication (AAC):
Part B: Literacy Skills and Instructional Goals	
Literacy Skills Include information on the learner's skills and indicate, if necessary, accommodations or modifications that may be needed to support physical or communication abilities	Book handling: Conventions of print: Phoneme-grapheme correspondence: Phonemic awareness: Phonics: Fluency: Vocabulary: Comprehension:
Relevant Grade-level literacy standard(s)	
Instructional Goals When developing goals, consider the five cross-cutting themes: meaning making, language development, effective expression, content knowledge, and foundational skills	(1) (2) (3)
Part C: Lesson Preparation	
Text Selection Consider student interests, home language and culture, grade-level books, current events, and experience books	Title of text:

Text Modification Based on the student's physical abilities, level of communication complexity, and sensory abilities identify the types of modifications to the text that are necessary to ensure optimal access to the content. For each modification checked, used the column to the right to describe the specific changes in detail	**Bypass Reading:** ❏ Change the modality ❏ Integrate AAC or technology **Decrease Reading:** ❏ Simplify vocabulary ❏ Change the storyline ❏ Decrease the amount of text ❏ Find an abridged version ❏ Simplify supplementary info **Support Reading:** ❏ Add repeated story line ❏ Add supplementary representations ❏ Objects ❏ Images ❏ Textures ❏ Other ❏ Enhance with textures ❏ Increase durability ❏ Add page turners **Guide & Organize Reading:** ❏ Graphic organizers ❏ Integrate multiple communication modes ❏ Structured notes	**Modification details:**
Learning Environment Ensure the learning environmental is intentionally arranged to support the learner's access and participation	Seating/positioning arrangements for the student: Classroom staff support during the activity: Ambient concerns:	

Part D: Literacy Instruction	
Prompting Identify prompts from each level to be used during instruction to support the learner	❏ The learner will **independently** respond without support **Auditory** / **Visual** / **Tactile** ❏ General verbal ❏ Gestural ❏ Partial physical ❏ Specific Verbal ❏ Photographic ❏ Full physical ❏ Model **Prompt detail:**
Target Vocabulary Identify high-utility terms from the text that can be generalized into other contexts and the specific communication mode from Part A that will be used for each to represent each term	**Vocabulary word** / **Representation** (blank rows)
Considerations for Vocabulary Instruction Ensure that provisions for instruction have been planned for prior to the start of the lesson	❏ Specific communication representations have been identified and created based on individual learner needs ❏ Speech Generating Devices have been programmed and loaded with key vocabulary for each learner ❏ Constant time delay interval has been determined that allows time for the learner to scan available choices and make a selection. Starting time interval: _____ seconds
Learner Attention and Prior Knowledge	Strategies for securing and maintaining learner attention: Strategies for activating prior knowledge:

Comprehension Questions Create questions using CROWD+ prompts with varied question styles should be varied. Include at least 5 questions in each set that will be alternated during repeated readings of the text	**LIST A** A1. A2. A3. A4. A5. A6.	**LIST B** B1. B2. B3. B4. B5. B6.

Appendix B
Interactive Reading Data Collection Sheet

Student:		Dates:	
Scorer:	Title:		Location:

Scoring: List the word or comprehension question on the designated list. At the start of the trial, enter the data at the top of the column. For each item, indicate the accuracy on the left side of the cell and level of independence or prompt provided on the right side.

Accuracy: ✗ correct and independent | **Prompt level:**
A – auditory V – visual T – tactile

Words	1	2	3	4	5	6	7	8	9	10
	| |	| |	| |	| |	| |	| |	| |	| |	| |	| |
	| |	| |	| |	| |	| |	| |	| |	| |	| |	| |
	| |	| |	| |	| |	| |	| |	| |	| |	| |	| |
	| |	| |	| |	| |	| |	| |	| |	| |	| |	| |
	| |	| |	| |	| |	| |	| |	| |	| |	| |	| |
	| |	| |	| |	| |	| |	| |	| |	| |	| |	| |
	| |	| |	| |	| |	| |	| |	| |	| |	| |	| |
	| |	| |	| |	| |	| |	| |	| |	| |	| |	| |
Graphing Circle the total number of correct and independent trials for each session then graph across all sessions.	8	8	8	8	8	8	8	8	8	8
	7	7	7	7	7	7	7	7	7	7
	6	6	6	6	6	6	6	6	6	6
	5	5	5	5	5	5	5	5	5	5
	4	4	4	4	4	4	4	4	4	4
	3	3	3	3	3	3	3	3	3	3
	2	2	2	2	2	2	2	2	2	2
	1	1	1	1	1	1	1	1	1	1

Appendix B: Interactive Reading Data Collection Sheet ♦ 137

Questions										
A	ǀ	ǀ	ǀ	ǀ	ǀ	ǀ	ǀ	ǀ	ǀ	ǀ
A	ǀ	ǀ	ǀ	ǀ	ǀ	ǀ	ǀ	ǀ	ǀ	ǀ
A	ǀ	ǀ	ǀ	ǀ	ǀ	ǀ	ǀ	ǀ	ǀ	ǀ
A	ǀ	ǀ	ǀ	ǀ	ǀ	ǀ	ǀ	ǀ	ǀ	ǀ
A	ǀ	ǀ	ǀ	ǀ	ǀ	ǀ	ǀ	ǀ	ǀ	ǀ
A	ǀ	ǀ	ǀ	ǀ	ǀ	ǀ	ǀ	ǀ	ǀ	ǀ
B	ǀ	ǀ	ǀ	ǀ	ǀ	ǀ	ǀ	ǀ	ǀ	ǀ
B	ǀ	ǀ	ǀ	ǀ	ǀ	ǀ	ǀ	ǀ	ǀ	ǀ
B	ǀ	ǀ	ǀ	ǀ	ǀ	ǀ	ǀ	ǀ	ǀ	ǀ
B	ǀ	ǀ	ǀ	ǀ	ǀ	ǀ	ǀ	ǀ	ǀ	ǀ
B	ǀ	ǀ	ǀ	ǀ	ǀ	ǀ	ǀ	ǀ	ǀ	ǀ
B	ǀ	ǀ	ǀ	ǀ	ǀ	ǀ	ǀ	ǀ	ǀ	ǀ
Graphing Circle the total number of correct and independent trials for each session then graph across all sessions.	6	6	6	6	6	6	6	6	6	6
	5	5	5	5	5	5	5	5	5	5
	4	4	4	4	4	4	4	4	4	4
	3	3	3	3	3	3	3	3	3	3
	2	2	2	2	2	2	2	2	2	2
	1	1	1	1	1	1	1	1	1	1

For Product Safety Concerns and Information please contact our EU
representative GPSR@taylorandfrancis.com
Taylor & Francis Verlag GmbH, Kaufingerstraße 24, 80331 München, Germany

www.ingramcontent.com/pod-product-compliance
Lightning Source LLC
Chambersburg PA
CBHW070403240426
43661CB00056B/2515